# Communication Odysseys

**Stuart Lenig**

**Lacey Benns**

**Daniel Johnson**
COLUMBIA STATE COMMUNITY COLLEGE

**KENDALL/HUNT PUBLISHING COMPANY**
4050 Westmark Drive    Dubuque, Iowa 52002

Copyright © 2005 by Kendall/Hunt Publishing Company

ISBN 0-7575-2273-4

All rights reserved. No part of this publication may be reproduced, stored in a retrieval system, or transmitted, in any form or by any means, electronic, mechanical, photocopying, recording, or otherwise without the prior written permission of the copyright owner.

Printed in the United States of America
10 9 8 7 6 5 4 3 2 1

# Contents

**Chapter 1  COMMUNICATION HISTORY                                    1**
Early Communication   1
Timeline   2
Later Classical Rhetoric   8
Later Rhetoric: The 18th Century   14
American System   14
How We Communicate Now   19

**Chapter 2  COMMUNICATION PHILOSOPHY                                23**
Introduction   23
Can We Talk?   24
Your Declaration of Independence   26
Is the "F" Word Gripping U?   27
So, Who Are U?   28
Everyone Has a Story. What's Yours?   29
Why Are U Here?   31
Great Philosophers Who Pondered Life   32
Back to U and Your Existence   32

**Chapter 3  COMMUNICATION MODELS                                    37**
Linear Models   37
Interactive Models   38
Transactional Model   38
Applying the Knowledge   41
Psychology and Communication   41
Political Communication Models   43
Media and Models   45

**Chapter 4  COMMUNICATION AND THE PERFORMANCE        51**
A Stage Is a Stage Is a Stage   52
Stars of the Stage and Screen Who Followed Those
    Nasty, Articulate Ancient Greeks and Romans   57
Coming Back to U   59

**Chapter 5  COMMUNICATION AND RESEARCH                       63**
Getting Started   63
Analyzing Your Audience   68

Visual Aids   69
Delivery of Speeches   70

**Chapter 6   COMMUNICATION AND INFORMING   75**
Introduction   75
Audience Analysis   75
Masters of Informative Speaking   76
Informative Speaking   77
Types of Speeches   78
Rhetorical Modes   80
Patterns   81
Speaking and Storytelling   83
The Philosophy of Informing   84

**Chapter 7   COMMUNICATION AND PERSUADING   89**
Critical Thinking   89
Decision Making   94
Orwell and Persuasion   99

**Chapter 8   COMMUNICATION INTERPERSONALLY   101**
Defining Interpersonal Communication   101
Verbal Communication   104
Nonverbal Communication   104
Listening   107
Important Communication Practices   109

**Chapter 9   COMMUNICATION INTERCULTURALLY   113**
Defining Culture   114
Subcultures   118
Understanding Culture   120
Applying Our Knowledge   121

**Chapter 10   COMMUNICATION AND THE MEDIA   125**
Introduction   125
The History of the Media (The History of the Entity That Made Britney Spears a Star)   125
The Camera: Picture This!   130
The Telephone: Honey, Ma Bell's Calling!   131
The Radio: Turn Your Radio On   132
The Television: A Tube for Boobs   134
Media Madness and U   136

**Chapter 11 COMMUNICATION AND POPULAR CULTURE 137**

Popular Culture   137
Youth Culture   140
Television Talk   140
Cartoon Talk: Simpsons, Bevis, and South Park   144
Music Talk   144
Film Speak: *Star Wars: Revenge of the Force:* 30 Years of Star Wars   146

**Chapter 12 COMMUNICATION AND CORRECT FORMAT 151**

Speaking and Writing Conventions: MLA and APA Styles   151
Using the MLA Format in Writing and Speaking   154
Citing Sources   154

# Chapter 1
## Communication History

In this chapter we will chart the progress of the field of communication. Recognize that communication is used today in at least two different ways. In ancient times communication or rhetoric was one's skill in public address to convince. Today it is widely considered an area of social science, the interaction psychologically and sociologically of people, groups and media. In this brief history of communication we will talk about both the rhetoric that famous people employed in their personal communication and the broader sociological communication that affected and changed society through the centuries.

## EARLY COMMUNICATION

Communication is not just a dead subject of "how to speak properly," or some simple rules for public address. Communication is as old as mankind itself. The root of oral communication began with Indo-European, the proto-language of all world languages. This language, linguists believe was the emergent language, the common root of all languages. This explains the common words in many other languages.

Anthropologists believe written language originated as a way to remember, transmit, or express spoken ideas. With writing you could take an idea across miles, remember, and recast it should the need arise. As in ancient times, the education of the young was as it is today conducted through oral communication. In Socrates time, the teacher would stand or sit amongst the students and lecture or speak at them. The forms of education included religious training, professional education (doctors, business, agricultural) and basic skills (writing, reading or math). Because all you needed was to have a pupil and instructor in the same room, education could happen at home, in meetings, or in ceremonies.

### Egypt to Rosetta Stone

The earliest written records we have of this style of education is in Egyptian hieroglyphic inscriptions. The key to the meaning of these hieroglyphics came rather late. Because the hieroglyphic language was lost after the ancient Egyptian culture declined and people began to speak what became modern day Arabic, no one was able to read the hieroglyphs for

# TIMELINE

- **2,000 BC** Papyrus Egyptian Culture
- **850 BC** Homer's *The Iliad* and *The Odyssey*: Achilles: Doer of Deeds/Speaker of Words
- **604–531 BC (?)** Lao Tsu Chinese philosopher
- **534 BC** First dramatic competition in Greece
- **500–300 BC** Greek Golden Age
- **495–426 BC** Greek Age of Pericles
- **465 BC** Corax: First Book of Rhetoric
- **431–404 BC** Peloponnesian Wars
- **436-338 BC** Isocrates School of Rhetoric
- **384–322 BC** Aristotle: *The Rhetoric*, the most influential book of rhetoric of all time!
- **335 BC** Aristotle's Poetics
- **200 BC-300 AD** Roman Empire
- **106-43 BC** Cicero great orator in the classical Roman Period
- **0–100 AD** Quintillian: "good man, speaking well"
- **410** Sack of Rome
- **500–1200** Traveling scholars, monks, Jews, Arabs preserve rhetorical training
- **700** Beowulf composed
- **1215** Magna Carta: Runnymeade, England
- King John/Parliament
- **1275** Edward I allows tradesmen in government
- **1372** Black Death appears in India
- **1429** Plautus Roman comedies rediscovered/Renaissance
- **1450** Gutenburg: Moveable type printing
- **1454** *The Bible* by Gutenburg, the first best seller!
- **1469** Lorenzo de Medici rules Florence
- **1450–1650** Rhetoric Schools flourish in Italy under patronage of nobles
- **1483–1546** Martin Luther German Protester: Founder of Protestant movement
- **1491–1547** Henry VIII: Enlightened monarch and failure of his administration
- **1533–1603** Elizabeth I: A real enlightened monarch, literate, and patron of the art
- **1588** Defeat of the Spanish Armada
- **1590–1613:** Shakespeare active
- **1600** Hamlet
- **1611** *King James Bible*
- **1642–1660** English Civil War
- **1700–1800** The Elocutionists
- **1776** Declaration of Independence: Revolutionary Movement
- **1789** French Revolution: Revolutionary Movement
- Deaths of Louis XVI (1792); Marat (1793); Danton (1794); Robspierre (1794)
- Reign of Terror
- **1799** Napoleon named First Consul of France.

| | |
|---|---|
| 1811–12 | Luddite riots in the North and the Midlands. Laborers attack factories |
| 1830 | Manchester Liverpool Railway (first in England) |
| 1828 | Noah Webster's *American Dictionary of the English Language* |
| 1849 | Gold discovered in California and Australia |
| 1850 | Telegraph cable laid under English Channel |
| 1851 | Great Exhibition ("Crystal Palace") |
| 1861 | Albert dies: Victoria retires into mourning |
| 1861–5 | American Civil War |
| 1869 | Union Pacific Railway completed in U.S. |
| 1876 | Edison invents the phonograph |
| 1879 | Edison invents the lightbulb |
| 1895 | U.S. equals the U.K.'s industrial output |
| 1900–1950 | *Life, Time, New York Times*, etc. establish journalism standards in America |
| 1914–18 | The "Great War" (World War I). |
| 1914 | *Birth of a Nation* |
| 1920 | KDKA: Pittsburgh radio station signs on the air |
| 1922 | Irish Free State established |

James Joyce: *Ulysses*

T.S. Eliot: *The Waste Land*

| | |
|---|---|
| 1929–40 | The Great Depression |
| 1933–1945 | FDR is President: The New Deal transforms America |
| 1939–45 | World War II |
| 1940 | *Citizen Kane* |
| 1946 | Expansion of television |
| 1960–1980 | Black English vernacular studied intensively |
| 1960 | Nixon-Kennedy debates |
| 1967 | *Sgt. Pepper*/Summer of Love |
| 1971 | *All in the Family* |
| 1974 | Watergate Impeachment |
| 1980 | CNN begins broadcasting |

Oprah Winfry transforms TV talk

| | |
|---|---|
| 1981 | MTV begins broadcasting |
| 1985 | Live Aid: Woodstock of the 80s on television |
| 1990 | Most American homes wired for cable, VCRs common appliance |
| 1992–2000 | Clinton Presidency, great prosperity |
| 2001 | WTC/Pentagon plane bombing |

Rhetoric of Revenge triggers Homeland Security/Afghan War/Iraq War

| | |
|---|---|
| 2002: | Investigation of Intelligence failure, Enron/Anderson/Stock Scandal |
| 2003: | Iraq War begins |
| 2004: | Kerry/Bush debates: Kerry wins debates/Bush wins election |

Martha Stewart jailed for "simple personal matter"

Photo courtesy of Photos.com

almost two thousand years. But in 1799, Napoleon's troops ran across an ancient stone while making their conquest of the world. The soldiers had the sense to realize they had discovered something valuable from the past. The stone, an ancient marker, contained three languages, one the heretofore untranslatable hieroglyphics and another which was the well known version of ancient Greek which scholars had long ago deciphered. This was the key to understanding the past. Speech was used in ancient cultures for education, day-to-day communication and public ceremonies, particularly amongst the upper classes.

## *Greece: Foundations of Rhetoric*

It was the Greeks who transformed the art of speech into a high form of discipline. In the period of the great Greek classical age from 500 B.C. to 300 B.C. the Greeks formalized rules for speech. But even earlier the Greeks were eloquent practitioners of the verbal arts. As far back as Homer's *Iliad*, written around 850 B.C., 350 years before the dawn of the Golden age of Greek culture, Homer was writing about the remarkable sophistication of Greek elocution. Here we see a formalized style of public address already in existence. In the epic poem, the character of Achilles is described partly by his rhetorical skills. He is called a "speaker of words and a doer of deeds." Words are here put on a par with actions suggesting that Greeks of that era held a man's word to be as important as his actions.

---

### OEDIPUS AND FREUD

The past still haunts us and dictates how we see the next generation. In terms of communication, the symbol of Oedipus the questioner, the seeker, the questor who turns out to be the murderer of his own father is reinvented by Freud in the 20th century. He is seen not as a clever man tricked by gods, but as a neurotic with unresolved urges to bond with his mother. Though many of Freud's observations about people and the world were colored by his own very repressive Victorian youth, many of Freud's ideas and images captivate modern people looking for a scientific way to explain the unknowable parts of our mind. Today the funniest readings of Freud come from feminist scholars who take issue with Freudian ideas such as penis envy and a woman's failure to gain power or resolve neuroses.

In the 9th book of *The Iliad* Achilles addresses three speakers/orators. Each is coming to Achilles tent to request his services. They wish him to get up and fight for the Athenians against the Trojans. Achilles is sulking and each tries in his own way to rouse the dejected warrior. The most successful and complicated of these addresses is that given by Odysseus, the most cunning and wily of the Greeks. You might recall that later in the war, it is Odysseus' plan to make the Trojan horse. Odysseus' address follows a five part form.

<u>Odysseus: Format of the Address</u>
1. Proemium: Greeting
2. Proposition: Point
3. Narrative: Background
4. Command: Action
5. Proof: Reasons

He begins with the proemium, a greeting to get Achilles' attention and goodwill. This is followed by the proposition or the reason for speaking. In essence, "Achilles we want you to come out and fight." This is followed by the narrative/exposition and background data in which Odysseus brings Achilles up to speed on what's been going on in the war in his absence. It isn't a pretty picture. This is followed by the command in which Odysseus orders or asks Achilles to obey his will. Finally he gives five reasons (proof) to support his claim. They fall under five categories.

1. Ethical reasons (you are one of us)
2. Authoritative (you should obey your commanders)
3. Inducements (look at the loot you can steal, the women you can have)
4. Pity and glory (take pity on your people who struggle in your absence and think of the glory you'll get for helping us)
5. Revenge (you can murder the mighty Hector, the Trojan hero who has made fun of you). Other addresses are made by Greek heroes Phoenix and Ajax, but none are so compelling as Odysseus' use of persuasive rhetoric.

The Greeks sculpted their society on the basis of informed talk. Why? When other cultures settled things with fists and weapons, why did the Greeks believe in talk? Part of the Greek interest in talk came from their geography. Greece was a place aptly suited to socialization. In fact, it was suited to little else. A group of islands apart from one another were not conducive to a centrally ruled government, nor were they well situated for conquest. They were rocky areas with little farm land and few marketable crops. What people could do was fish, raise grape vines, herd sheep and sail. Thus, the Greeks were left with a lot of time on their hands.

They had a simple frugal diet, and they had each other and that was about it. To make things happen they had to be creative and invent things, like intricate rules for the use of oral language. If talk is all you have, you learn to study it or life becomes incredibly boring doesn't it? So the Greeks became clever talkers, writers, historians, observers, sailors and tradesmen. Although Greece had a slave culture it was generally a place of egalitarian principles, the birthplace of democracy, the place where people spoke to get office. Democracy itself means people (demos) as ruler (crates). In the most democratic state, Athens, citizens ruled by direct town meetings.

Socrates:      480–399 B.C.
Plato:         427–347 B.C.
Aristotle:     384–322 B.C.
Alexander:     356–323 B.C.

The Athenian achievement was to create the first formal persuaders. Corax in 465 B.C. wrote the first book on the subject. The concept of small group discussion took root. Through the geographic limitations of empire, Greeks learned complex rules and skills for conducting organized discussion to get things done. They practiced what is known as the Socratic method, so named for its creator Socrates. He would ask questions of his students and expect a reply, a practice that is still observed in our schools today and the form that our legal address takes in a court of law.

While the method of question and answer was generally a positive thing there was a down side to living by the word. We have the practice of the Marathon runner who today runs 26 miles. In Greek times, the Marathon runner would be sent back to the court to tell the outcome of the battle. Often the stress and energy exerted to bring the news home would kill the runner. Another problem was the practice of "killing the messenger," literally murdering the fellow that brought you bad news, not a particularly encouraging practice for good reporting.

Even after the decline of Greek culture, Greek learning was highly prized and incorporated into the Roman educational system. The two parts of the classical curriculum included the trivium and quadrivium derived directly from Greek education. Essential components of this educational plan included: math, gymnastics, rhetoric, and music. Rhetoric as it was practiced in ancient times was not just talk aimed at convincing or

## DIOGENES AND ALEXANDER

Now in Ancient Greece, you did not have to be wealthy to be famous. In fact, the poorest man about was probably the most controversial and most courted. His name was Diogenes and he was responsible for a brand of philosophy known as cynicism but it could have just as easily been called skepticism because Diogenes was eternally skeptical of all government, religious, or social laws that bound men by foolish and conventional wisdom and did not depend on outside verification. Diogenes lived in a big terra cotta greek urn or vase that he slept in like a dog house. He had one possession other than this, a cloak that he used as a toga, a blanket and a weapon to chase away intruders. But despite his idiosyncratic lifestyle, Diogenes was often sought for his untainted advice. After all, since he owned nothing and sought only truth he was certainly reliable. Diogenes' brand of cynicism was known as doggishness because like a dog that pulls on a rope toy or bone, the dog and Diogenes was often more interested in the game of finding truth than the ultimate outcome.

Diogenes was famous for exploits. He would defecate in the streets, beg for food and harass the populace. One month he walked around with an old oil lantern and carried the lighted lamp in broad daylight peering into the faces of the wealthy and powerful. Finally, one man boldly asked him what he was looking for, and Diogenes said: "An honest man." When Athens was preparing for war and people began scurrying all over the place making preparations, securing food, tying down loose buildings, Diogenes began to roll his bedroom/urn up a steep hill again and again. Each time he'd allow it to roll down and start the whole process again. The people were puzzled since they felt he should be making a practical contribution to the war effort. "What are you doing Diogenes, why are you rolling that urn up the hill?" Diogenes looked at them and said, "well since you were all so busy working hard at your activities, I thought I'd better get busy too." Of course Diogenes was lightly poking fun at the people for working so seriously at preparations for war, the most destructive and pointless of human enterprises.

One day, Alexander the Great, the conqueror who had taken control of Greece came to town. His lords and attendants asked him what he wished in the town. Alexander, schooled by Aristotle was no fool and he said he had come to seek wisdom. He asked to speak to Diogenes, but his friends sought dissuade him, knowing Diogenes' reputation for brutal honesty, they were not sure the young king could tolerate the old cynic. Finally, Alexander prevailed on them to take him to Diogenes' street corner and reluctantly the retinue brought Alexander to the old man, swatting flies on his back and sitting in the gutter. Alexander came down from his chariot to chat with the old man who kept his back turned to Alexander. Alexander, ever gracious and ingratiating tried to engage the elder philosopher. Is there anything I can do for you Diogenes?" he asked genuinely. Diogenes spoke without looking up. "Yes, you can move your blocking my light." The group of nobles was stunned and momentarily fearful. After a moment Alexander broke into broad laughter, returned to his chariot and departed. Later, his lords asked him what he thought of the conversation. Alexander responded, "If I were not Alexander, I would be Diogenes." Alexander knew of Diogenes wisdom that only the poor and honest philosopher or the world ruler could truly speak his mind.

winning over an opposing side, it was an interdisciplinary practice incorporating: history, philosophy, grammar, and human nature (psychology) into the study of speaking.

One of the great rhetoricians of the period was Isocrates (436-338 BC), no relation to the philosopher, Socrates. Isocrates opened a school to teach rhetoric, and he worked as a speechwriter to support himself. His school had a stable location at a time when many teachers were wandering professors going from town to town to make a living. He supervised the development of his students and he demanded self-discipline in their study. Not only did he create the curriculum of his school, but because he lived a long and fruitful life he was able to monitor the curriculum for over 50 years. Besides teaching speech, he also gave some famous addresses, among the most famous was his speech: Against the sophists. The sophists were instructors and intellectuals who taught at schools but focused on rhetorical tricks in order to win arguments. For them argument was a game, not a quest for truth and accurate knowledge.

Isocrates view of a great rhetorician was a combination of these elements: nature, practice and training. To Isocrates great rhetoricians were supposed to be seeking philosophy and knowledge. Underlying great speakers, in his mind, were qualities of moral character which cannot be taught. Isocrates left us no text, but that universal Greek thinker Aristotle did. His *The Rhetoric* became the bible of public speaking for over 2,000 years. He broke the subject of rhetoric into parts. (Aristotle was good at organizing, analyzing and dividing.) Rhetoric required five skills to Aristotle. These were:

1. finding and supporting a subject
2. organizing the topic for greatest effect
3. using an appropriate level/style of expression
4. expert delivery for clarity and impact
5. use of events (examples, facts, colorful information) to make memorable.

Aristotle's achievement was to codify all the practices of rhetoric that were existing in his day into a clear and reasonable book that almost anyone could apply to their speaking.

## LATER CLASSICAL RHETORIC

The Sophists (the Greek word sophos meaning wise) was actually in rhetoric a negative term denoting superficial empty talk. As the Greek world declined and was absorbed into the Roman empire the practice of rhetoric was incorporated too.

Rome conquered Greece and as in all things with all cultures, the Romans were ingenious at incorporating those best elements of subjugated cultures into the basic Roman culture. Imagine how we as Americans do the same thing today. We aren't particularly Chinese in our world view, but we can incorporate ancient Chinese thought into our culture. Michael Douglas in the movie *Wall Street* continually quotes Sun Tzu on *The Art of War*. We don't have an indigenous tradition of martial arts in America but in *Kung-Fu*, David Carradine plays a man who practices this self-defense technique. The show has been a hit in syndication for 20 years. Like the Romans we practice cultural sampling as a positive quality.

In Rome, Greek tutors taught rhetoric to Roman youth to improve their speaking abilities. Roman institutions used the format of rhetorical address. The Forum where people would argue matters of politics was a means of debating in public. One of the most notable Roman rhetoricians was Cicero who spoke in the Senate and was later murdered. Quintillian was a great codifier of rhetorical ideas and wrote books on the subject of Rhetoric.

In Quintillian's rhetoric (derived directly from Aristotle) there were five canons or laws:

1. invention
2. organization
3. style
4. memory
5. delivery

Today, our texts in speech and communication are still based on Greek and Roman principles.

## *Non-Western Communication*

Zen Buddhist teaching emphasizes the Zen koan or story of philosophical import. In many such stories a teacher sits either puzzling, challenging or actually beating students to help them to achieve a deeper understanding of their world. There are many great zen stories of philosophical import that are taught to create better reasoning and moral principles simultaneously. We unfortunately tend to focus either on morality of intellect usually at the expense of one or the other. Perhaps the Asian scholars have something.

Rhetoric was practiced in a philosophical manner throughout Southeast Asia. Lao-Tsu practiced a Chinese rhetoric that became the Tao te Ching, a famous text of philosophical enquiry. In Japan Shotetsu Mongatari and Seami practiced the art of Japanese rhetoric.

## *The Power of Metaphor*

Just because official western culture practices a certain form of rhetoric is no reason to assume that other cultures lack in an understanding of language used to persuade and inform. Native American and African cultures are rich in non-literary storytelling traditions. In Joseph Campbell's

> **THE OLD WARRIOR**
>
> There was once an old warrior who had endured countless battles and never been felled by an opponent. He had in later years become a great teacher of younger warriors, and they were beloved students who cherished the old man's wisdom. One day, a nasty young warrior with a fearsome reputation for besting all opponents with his brutal attack came to the school to meet and beat the master in competition. Much to the fear of his students the old warrior agreed to fight with the savage young warrior. The students begged him to reconsider but he came out to battle. The young hot-headed warrior was keen to perceive the mistakes and weaknesses of all enemies, and he was a master at exploiting any weakness he found. A principle weapon was inducing fear and anger in his opponents thus making them lose control and think with their emotions instead of their intellect. He came before the old man. He smiled.
> "You are much smaller and shorter than I had heard."
> The old warrior stood alert and resolute. He said nothing.
> "Your wisdom was proclaimed to me by all but you have said nothing that impresses me. Tired and worn out old man? Too tired to speak?"
> Again, the old warrior said or did nothing.
> The young warrior continued his verbal assaults calling the older man names, spitting on him and kicking dust in his face with his sword.
> Throughout it all the old man held his ground and stood without movement or reaction.
> Eventually, the young man knew he was losing the battle and would not be able to defeat the old man. "You are nothing but a coward. You waste my time and energy. There are younger men I could defeat rather than wasting time here." With that he gave a last spit towards the old man and departed in disgrace and aware that he was unable to find any crack in the old man's mental armor.
> If you were a zen warrior, what would you make of this story?

*Power of Myth* he describes the power of myth to transform our everyday world. Storytelling survives as an art and communication form. Storytelling is an excellent means of providing a moral or philosophical lesson without having to make direct pronouncements. Today in the U.S. mountain regions there are still famous and successful storytellers, and there are even competitions amongst storytellers in rural regions.

This form has been appropriated in the mass media entertainment field as the variety show, the stand up routine and the comedy performer. Why do people go to see comedians except to be told humorous stories?

In fact, storytelling has inspired great literature. In Ray Bradbury's *Fahrenheit 451*, firemen of the future burn books, and the rebels of this time have to become living books: learning, reciting, and retelling books over and over again, to keep knowledge alive and growing. Today, Native American folk tales have been used to bind the Native American culture together and to provide for the culture's survival in an age when this culture might have perished and become totally absorbed.

## The Dark Ages

Between the fall of the Roman empire and the Renaissance, there was a time when knowledge was imperiled by no strong central organized governmental force. Knowledge was preserved by several brave sources. European monasteries in Western Europe preserved knowledge through printing illustrated books and living a self-contained Spartan existence with little contact from the outside world. These illuminated manuscripts assumed that the populace was mostly illiterate and provided text and pictures to render biblical stories more accessible. Much of the knowledge of the Ancient world was preserved in Arab universities and libraries which thrived from the time of Mohammed until the end of the middle ages. Jewish settlements around the world had communities of scholars who kept and preserved knowledge.

In this time, large masses of people began to congregate and live in towns moving from an agrarian to a merchant culture. There emerged a need for mass communication. The first example of this was the town crier. The preacher or priest gained power because most people were illiterate and could not read *The Bible* for themselves. Still, there were pockets of knowledge. Isidore of Spain, a Jewish teacher who wrote about clear order and style preserved the study of Rhetoric in this dark time.

## Renaissance

Finally, the city states of Italy came into being. Trade was generating new information and the Italian seamen were rediscovering ancient knowledge, literally there was a rebirth or renaissance of knowledge, a re-emergence of information.

Rhetoric returned in schools. Italian schools modeled on city states of Greece and Rome were funded by rich families who patronized the arts and culture as an advertisement for themselves. The Borgias, Medicis and Zforzas all wanted glory and power. In 1450 the technological breakthrough of moveable type printing began. Although others may have begun before him, Johann Gutenberg is credited with the innovation and his *Bible* in 1454 was the first best seller. Finally, people could have relatively cheap and inexpensive copies of religious texts in their own homes. An immediate outgrowth was more freethinking. People began to question the church and its authority. This was something the church didn't like because authority and power was a good thing to have in order to control people.

The printing press also began modern scholarship. People who could read and write could compare ideas and choose which ones to accept and believe. People's worlds suddenly became much bigger. An advantage of print was that ideas could be more effectively presented. Martin Luther was the first religious reformer to be widely published which gave him broad influence. He was actually able to confront the authority of the Church.

## MARTIN LUTHER BEFORE THE DIET OF WORMS IN 1521 (ABRIDGED)

Photo courtesy of Library of Congress

The leader of the German Protestant Reformation was called before the Emperor, Charles V to answer a Papel Bull (message) in which the Pope had asked to have Luther brought to Rome (most certainly to be tried and killed for heresy). Charles the V and the German nobles had good reason to hear Luther out. He offered them solid theological grounds to get out from under the thumb of the Pope and obtain greater secular power. Luther for his side had presented his theses against Catholic indulgences in the spirit of a good social reformer and his cause seemed just.

Two questions were asked of me yesterday, by his imperial highness; the first was whether I was the author of the books that were described; the second was whether I wished to renounce or defend the doctrine I have taught. I answered the first question, and I stand by that answer.

As for the second question, I have composed writings on a variety of different subjects. In some articles I have discussed Faith and Good Deeds, in a spirit so totally pure, clear and Christian, that even my foes can find nothing objectionable and confess that these writings are excellent exemplums for devout people. The pope's Bull, violent as it is, admits to this. What would happen if I were to retract these writings? Miserable man! I alone would be abandoning the truth proclaimed by my friends and enemies, and would oppose doctrines that the whole world praises and glorifies.

**Questions on Content**

1. What has Luther been accused of according to this text?
2. Why do you suppose the Pope is angry about Luther's writings?

**Questions on Form**

1. How does Luther manage to be direct and eloquent simultaneously?
2. What sort of structure can you see Luther employing?

**Vocabulary**

Papal Bull
Faith and Good Deeds
doctrine
renounce
recant

In England Henry VIII, the first monarch to be educated through the new technology of literacy joined in questioning through the use of new knowledge. He rejected the power of the pope and the existing church and started his own church, the Church of England, under his own secular command although ostensibly administered and given divine guidance by the Archbishop of Canterbury. This action would have been impossible if Henry hadn't been aware of his power and the limitations of Roman authority through the use of printed data. Henry learned he could rebel, that it was possible, and he did.

But the English had been rebellious against their own government much earlier when the nobles banned together against their King in 1215 and forced then king, King John to sign the Magna Carta, the earliest British proto-bill of rights for Englishmen.

The British quickly moved to establish a ruling body to make sure the King had some control over his decision making. They established the Parliament (from French parler, meaning "to speak"). This was a place where the nobles and king could speak and discuss their opposing viewpoints. In 1275 Edward the first included merchants along with the rich in government. Parliament became a place to debate. It developed into two houses, the House of Commons for commoners, and the house of Lords for noblemen. This institution was the forerunner of the American Congress, the House and the Senate.

Mostly British debate was spirited but not violent, but in the English revolution of 1642–1660, the Puritans allowed the inclusion of the common people in the running of the government. British debate has remained world famous for its use of language, its continued ability to discuss important issues in a rational manner and its adherence to sound logical principles in a free society.

## LATER RHETORIC: THE 18TH CENTURY

By the 1700s some of the emphasis on content in speaking had been replaced by an emphasis on form. The Elocutionist movement (1700–1800): favored (a) grand gesture, (b) elegant vocabulary, (c) flowing vocal tones. These qualities dominated speaking and the content of addresses and argument were neglected in favor of stylistic matters. Today, we would find the Elocutionists interest in correct speech wholly academic.

### Revolutionary Tradition

Numerous speakers have been impelled to speak by the revolutionary tradition which arose in direct contrast to the Elocutionists. Where the Elocutionists favored correctness of form over content, the Revolutionary speakers have always been much more audience-centered giving a message that would arouse and provoke an audience rather than worrying about matters of style. When Patrick Henry spoke to the Virginia Convention of Delegates, he was exciting an audience through his charged words. His rhetorical questions stung. "Is life so dear, or peace so sweet, as to be purchased at the price of chains and slavery? Forbid it Almighty God!"

When Vladimir Lenin aroused the proletariat, he touched a cord of anger that laid deep within the Russian people from years of oppression under the repressive czarist regimes. Napoleon encouraging his troops in Europe, Castro in the hills of Cuba and Vaclav Havel speaking to the people from prison or the streets of Prague all accomplished their revolutions through their use of words.

## AMERICAN SYSTEM

Today, we use words in many ways, to sell, convince, amuse and explain. One of the hallmarks of the American system is our right of free speech, the first amendment to the constitution. Authoritarian governments limit the free expression of ideas, because free thinking can endanger the status quo. Our system has actually revolution and renewal from within which has helped to keep the American system of government healthier than some would-be democracies.

Where some societies actually limit the amount of ideas to be accepted and debated, our society allows for a greater tolerance of a wide variety of ideas. In fact our tolerance for a wide diversity of fringe views

## GEORGE WASHINGTON: THE MAN WHO WOULD NOT BE KING

At the end of the revolutionary war, many in the revolutionary army were concerned that civil government could not govern effectively. They feared that civil governments were weak and that although they had feared the authority of King George III of England, maybe a king and monarchy was the proper form of government. England had tried a republican monarchy one hundred years earlier and Cromwell's disastrous reign resulted in a return to monarchy and a new form of constitutional government. A letter was sent to Washington asking him to take charge of the government and to usurp the civil authority of the continental congress. Washington was being called upon to become a dictator and a king. Washington was faced with a terrible choice. After exhausting himself and the resources of the nation in a ten year struggle against the English, Washington was being asked to betray the revolution and become a king, something he abhorred. Washington had to go before his troops, the brave soldiers he had fought beside for a decade and either accept their offer of revolution or decline and throw the nation into a chaotic power struggle. The defectors had their reasons. Congress had refused to pay soldiers who had fought bravely against the British. They bickered and governed willfully and often unwisely.

Washington drew himself together and wrote a speech responding to their offer. He gave his reasons for why he could not accept such an offer, and how the betrayal of the revolution by a counter revolution pained him. He could feel that he was losing the audience. They were not impressed by his lofty rhetoric and his noble thoughts. Instead, they were bitter and resentful and angry. Washington judged the mood of his men. He saw that his approach to reason and logic, to logos was a failure. He needed to address their ethos and pathos concerns, their ethical and emotional feelings. He put aside his speech and looked at the men in an understanding and heartfelt way. He smiled at the men and stopped to read them a letter from a widow who had a lost a loved one in the war. However, Washington's sight was deteriorating and he required glasses to read the letter. He pulled out some wire rimmed spectacles and donned them. Along with his black hair that had greyed, Washington, rather than a dramatic general and leader now appeared a gentle grandfatherly figure. The men were stunned. They had never seen Washington looking so old, so frail, and so vulnerable. He realized the power of his look and of his aged appeal. He spoke to them. "You must excuse me, gentlemen, not only have I grown grey in the service of my country, I have also grown blind."

The men were heartsick at their disloyalty to the nation and particularly to the man they had watched share their suffering for the past decade. How could they betray so noble a revolution and so noble a man, a man who had given his mind, soul and body to the cause of freedom, and was so vulnerable before them. After hearing Washington's words, the counter-revolution dissolved, and the men devolved into sobs and tears weeping like babies before their leader. They were unwilling to continue with their plans to overthrow Congress. The revolution was saved by Washington because he refused to be the man who wanted to be king. The next year he was elected America's first president. Eventually, the revolutionary troops were paid. Congress still bickered and was often ineffective but the American system was saved from countless internal betrayals.

and bizarre ideas (cult religions, fringe political parties, odd marketing by unusual candidates) keeps revolutionary anger in check.

Free speech has had a remarkable and far reaching impact on American society. It has created presidents, changed social conditions (depression/the great society), started the civil rights movement, provided consumer protection (against commercial claims), raised public consciousness about dangerous social issues (Love Canal/Vietnam), created equality for all groups and given a voice to all people of all economic and social standings such as the great African-American speaker, Sojourner Truth. Truth was a woman born into slavery but after the Civil War she became a courageous and outspoken advocate of women's and African-American rights. In a famous encounter at a speaking hall, Truth was heckled by insensitive men who accused her of not even being female. She exposed her bosoms to the men to prove her femininity. The men left the room embarrassed and ashamed. She gave a fiery speech entitled "Ain't I a Woman" proclaiming the suffering of her life as a testimony to women's suffering under oppression and the dreadful conditions of slavery.

## *Speech Communication: A Discipline*

Rhetoric is more commonly called the more general term of speech or communication in the 20th century.

Photo courtesy of Library of Congress.

But back in the 19th century rhetoric was enjoying renewed academic prestige. John Harvard endowed a college in Cambridge, Massachusetts, and reversed an endowed chair in rhetoric. This "Boylston chair" created in 1806 set academic standards for the field of public address.

John Quincy Adams used the chair to promote classical rhetoric study. Professor Channing altered the focus of the chair to center on literary criticism. In the later twentieth century rhetoric became synonymous with composition. So much was the field of rhetoric identified with written address that today many English essay texts like ours are called "rhetorics."

So bad was the practice of rhetoric at the start of the 20th century that scholar/rhetorician I. A. Richards called rhetoric "the dreariest and least profitable part of the waste that the unfortunate travel through in Freshman English." To Richards, rhetoric had abdicated a principle part of its role as a means to shape thought and action. To use rhetoric was to use skills in argument, but to Richards it was much more. Rhetoric was not just persuasion. It was being able to "psych out" an audience. This involved understanding the people one was talking with and attempting to as Richards put it, please the imagination. A speaker would seek to move the passions by eliciting an emotional response. Logically the speaker would attempt to influence the will.

Another goal of speaking in Richard's thought was the speaker's use of language to produce understanding in the audience. In his writings, Richard's used the expressive vocabulary of poetry to describe the speaking process. The terms "sense, feeling, tone, and intention" are important to his view of the speaking experience. Kenneth Burke was another 20th century philosopher of rhetoric. His concept of the need for a speaker to make identification with the listeners in order to make the appeal. This causes the speaker to become what Burke called Consubstantial to the audience.

He described the speaking act as a dramatic pentad involving five elements:

1. Act
2. Agent
3. Agency (means)
4. Scene (background)
5. Purpose.

Although rhetoric was largely ignored during the early twentieth century, there was a resurgence from 1920–40. Cornell held a seminar in classical rhetoric in which the works of Aristotle, Cicero, and Quintillian were once again studied. Rhetorical analysis was used in the New Criticism style of literary criticism. New Criticism looked intently at the work itself internally to discover how a text operated.

Rhetoric also played a role in the burgeoning study of psychological/philosophical speculation. Chaim Perelman said that Descartian reality was not valuable for most people. We as people live in the probable, contingent, plausible world, but most of us do not think in terms of rational logical analysis. Perelman argued that non-formal logic, that is dialectical, Aristotelian proofs provided a better foundation for thinking. Perelman took a cue from legal thinking and applied the concept of precedent to his view of informal logic. For Perelman, a precedent is not absolute, just as a legal precedent can be reversed by a higher court. All a precedent can do is provide a reasonable basis for judgment. Thus to Perelman, social, psychological, and cultural conditions determine new ways of persuasion. For example, today we might be more persuaded to either approve or disapprove of a celebrity by what we read in a tabloid (a cultural device for getting news) and an interview television program (a psychological portrayal of a person) than by some formal logical analysis. The opinion of that person (precedent) might alter radically in a matter of months. Take any noteworthy celebrity: Madonna, Michael Jackson or Kevin Costner as an example of how quickly such opinions can change.

As an academic discipline, the old views of rhetoric as just good elocution were derided. Often rhetoric programs were absorbed into English departments where speech study was minimized. It was assumed that most communication would be conducted through written transmission rather than oral. While that still holds true today with an emphasis in our institutions on written versus vocal face-to-face rhetoric, technology is making verbal and oral persuasion paramount again. The aforementioned influence of the media with its emphasis on talk shows suggests that people don't necessarily trust reading anymore, but would rather talk out problems. Psychologists decry a failure of parents and children, spouses, genders, differing cultural and ethic groups, and generations to communicate. Employers won't hire communication illiterates. Our technology is changing quickly from text oriented to symbols to speech driven computers, media presentations, videos and other direct forms of address that do not require extensive written documentation. The growth of the internet with its mixture of text and pictures has helped to rebirth written culture as a significant medium.

The Speech Communication Association was started at the turn of the century to offer studies of speech and rhetoric in its increasingly interdisciplinary facets as a humanistic/scientific discipline, a science/social science/art form, a communicative behavior and in scholarly studies of allied areas such as classical rhetoric, theatre and mass communication. The society was renamed the National Communication Association. Now speech and communication have become careers of their own with many rhetoricians becoming active in the justice system, communication industries, speech writing, mass media, television, public relations, marketing, etc.

The New Rhetoric is a deeply interdisciplinary art involving psychology, semantics, motivational research, behavioral science as well as the traditional media of public address. Ironically, little has been mentioned about the role of women in rhetoric, although they have long been significant speakers and persuaders in the world arena. Truthfully, women were shut out of most of the history of rhetoric for some very sexist reasons. First they were denied access and secondly, not given formal education in the field. Men actively blocked their entrance to the field keeping it an all male domain.

Now feminist rhetoricians are making up for lost time. Camille Paglia in her book *Sexual Personae* makes some interesting analyses of women and woman's role in our culture. Germane Greer redefined women's roles in *The Female Eunuch*. Dr. Deborah Tannen's book entitled *You Just Don't Understand* illustrates that men and women don't even talk a truly common language. In fact the sexes use language quite differently.

All of this adds up to the field of rhetoric being a lively and exciting place for the next few years as the spoken word through cable, computers and popular culture wins back its rightful place in our culture.

## HOW WE COMMUNICATE NOW

Spoken communication may play a smaller part of the entire mix of communication formats. Where do people spend their time? Who do they listen to? Who do they talk to? Studies differ, but in an online study published by Roland Soong (2002), subjects revealed that well-educated, professional males tended to watch less than the average 4.3 hours of television a day and tended to utilize the internet more frequently. The suggestion is that the internet is used for more communication and television for that group remains a marginalized pursuit. A 2002 study from BIG Research indicated that multitasking was a

### Tabloid Culture: Oprah, Springer, and Fox News

Much has been made of the current state of discourse. For one thing, most discourse today is mediated by television, the internet or other mediums. It appears to be much easier to manipulate audiences with sensational stories rather than valuable and important data to make meaningful decisions. The Romans referred to this policy as "bread and circuses." If you could provide enough bread to feed the plebians and enough amusement to keep them sedated, the masses would pose no problem to the rulers. In Jeanette Walls' book, *Dish*, she describes the 20th century as an era of gossip talk and this era is certainly the land of tabloid lurid journalistic discourse. Americans may talk a lot, but they don't seem to talk about much.

In the 1950s, a man named Generoso Pope, Jr. started a tacky publication named *The National Enquirer*. It featured lurid stories on the deaths of Marilyn Monroe (the contents of her stomach on inside photos) and photos of the Kennedy assassination autopsy with plentiful pictures of the dead president minus his brain and half his head. Horrible but thrilling stuff, *The Enquirer* became a must read for many Americans. People would seek out *The Enquirer* on newsstands. But Pope wanted a newspaper that could be sold to women in supermarkets, so he toned down the violence and focused on more society and Hollywood scandals sans blood. But Pope was worried that his New York tabloid wasn't getting to the people. He suspected teamster corruption suppressing his magazine so he asked an old mob friend, Angie Pastornia to ride along with a delivery truck. The next day, Pastornia was found dead in a truck with a knife through him and a note that read, "Don't fuck with us." Pope called a meeting with Richard Nixon in Florida (Nixon was president at the time and had a home in Florida). Pope wanted to relocate his business there from out of New York and in exchange for his giving Nixon favorable coverage in *The National Enquirer*, Nixon promised to invite supermarket chain owners to the White House. He promised to persuade them to put the National Enquirer in their magazine racks. He did. They did, and to this day, *The National Enquirer* is a staple of most supermarket checkout lines.

The big success story of the seventies was *People Magazine*, a journal that dwelled on the private lives of celebrities. Not as lurid as *The Enquirer*, it was a gossip magazine that was launched by *Time* magazine. They thought of it as low journalism, but the debut issue had a great picture of Elizabeth Taylor. Usual issues of *Time* sold 35 percent of their copies. The first issue of *People* sold a phenomenal 85 percent of printed copies, due mainly to the connection between the subject matter and the television viewing of potential readers.

In the seventies, the Elvis death story became an enormously popular sleeze topic. The Memphis Mafia (Elvis friends and cronies) tried to weed out the reporters, but one celebrity reporter crept in without notice, Carolyn Kennedy. She wrote a dull story on the subject, but Jann Werner at *Rolling Stone*, saw the importance of the issue and immediately rewrote and published her story. Geraldo Rivera was working at ABC and created the news magazine, *20/20*, but he also did a story linking Marilyn Monroe to the Kennedys. This well documented story was killed by Roone Arledge, a producer who had dated Ethel Kennedy and had ties to Kennedy aides. Rivera was hired by ABC to cause controversy and when he found it, they dumped him.

Ironically one of the big manipulators of tabloid trash of the nineties according to Walls was Michael Jackson. He would offer stories such as he slept in an oxygen chamber to help preserve him to 150 years old. Or he would send in stories saying that Prince

**Communication History** 21

> was sending ESP messages to his chimp, Bubbles. He was reported to be bidding on the bones of the elephant man. Later, Jackson's strange relationship with the press would aid him in accusations of sexual misconduct with children. People that didn't believe the earlier stories were unlikely to believe the later misdeeds.
>
> The ultimate tabloid subject in the nineties was Princess Diana, often referred to as the tabloid princess. Her well publicized split with Prince Charles, her many post-Charles affairs were consistently covered by the press. She used her new found publicity to speak out on AIDS research and the plight of the poor. Whoever the subject is, tabloid journalism has changed who and what journalists cover as news. The subject of news in recent years is less world events and more individual social events.

growing means of utilizing media. More people (women were faster adaptors than men) were viewing television while interneting, reading a magazine while watching TV, and paging through a newspaper with a radio in the background. With only 24 hours in a day, people are seeking to communicate more in less time.

# Chapter 2

## Communication Philosophy

"Getting 2 No U—Getting 2 No All About U"

## Introduction

As I begin writing this chapter, I am visualizing U—whomever U may be—in my mind's eye. More than likely, U are a college student who must take a speech class in order to fulfill the requirements of your degree program. The book that U are now reading is the required text for the course. If U are like many of my former students—and U probably are—U are dreading this class. U do not understand why this is a required course. U are thinking: "How can taking a speech class possibly help me? I already know how to talk."

It's true; unless U have some type of physical impairment, U do know how to and can talk. Since U were a baby—perhaps as early as eight or nine months old—U have spoken words. Perhaps, your first words were something profound, like "Momma" or "Daddy." As U grew and your brain developed, U continued to discover the world around U and to learn the names—or **labels**—that have been given to things to help humans make sense of that world. U learned to tie your words together to make complete thoughts—sentences. U learned to speak these words—and sentences—in order to help U survive in an ever-changing world of thoughts and deeds; and, so far, U have survived. So, U are still thinking: "I have made it this far. Why are THEY requiring me to take this speech class?"

Photo courtesy of Photos.com

Speaking as one of the "THEYS" (professional educators), the answer is quite simple and stated in the form of a couple of questions to U. "Yes, U can talk; but do U really know how to **communicate?** And, if U do know how to talk so well, why are U dreading to stand up in front of your fellow-classmates in the near future and present your thoughts and ideas with them in a clear, concise manner? Why do U fear the "wonderful opportunity" to make a speech?

## CAN WE TALK?

The sad truth is that in the world in which U are living today, most people only know how to talk. They speak; but, their sentences have no substance. They talk to function—to survive. But, they really do not know how to effectively **communicate** their thoughts, feelings and ideas with others. Throughout the world, the results of this "failure to communicate" are scarred upon the lives of human beings. These communication "scars" are rooted in the history of mankind. Clear, concise verbal and/or written expressions of thoughts and ideas—as well as intentionally misspoken thoughts and ideas—have caused many family breakups; have determined political fates; have resulted in economic turmoil; and have caused countless wars in which millions of people have died.

In her thoroughly researched college textbook, **Interpersonal Communication—Everyday Encounters,** author Julia T. Wood cites a 1999 poll that reported that a majority of people in the United States believe that communication problems are the most common cause of divorce. In the poll, the research organization Roper Starch interviewed 1001 Americans, asking a variety of questions concerning the role of communication in their lives. Fifty-three percent of the interviewees stated that ineffective communication was the primary reason for divorce in the United States.

Politically-speaking, the fate of political candidates has lain in their abilities to clearly articulate and communicate their ideas and agendas. During the 2004 presidential campaign, Democratic Senator Howard Dean's much-televised, tirade of comments made during a campaign speech effectively eliminated him as a serious candidate during the Democratic primaries. Later that year, during the presidential debates, many Republican pundits expressed concern after the first debate after President George W. Bush performed poorly against his Democratic challenger, Senator John Kerry. Some of his staunchest supporters pointed out that President Bush appeared to be ill-prepared for the debate and did not seemed to be relaxed. Much to his party's pundits' collective relief, the President fared better against Senator Kerry in the second and third debates. Still, the pundits knew that if the President faltered in his ability to effectively communicate his ideas with the American people, the course of political history could have been changed.

Financially-speaking, the stability of the world's economy is dependent upon solid, factual information and communication. One of the most dramatic financial collapses in the history of corporate America was the demise of Enron. Many business analysts believe that Enron's demise was due to faulty corporate communication practices. In an article titled "Explaining Enron—Communication and Responsible Leadership" which was published in *Management Communication Quarterly, Vol. 17, No. 1,* (2003), Matthew W. Seeger of Wayne State University and Robert R. Ulmer of the University of Arkansas-Little Rock wrote a detailed analysis that explained Enron's demise by employing the principles of communication-based leader responsibilities. According to Seeger and Ulmer, these responsibilities include: (1) Recognizing and being open to signs of problems; (2) Communicating appropriate values that lead to the creation of a moral business climate; and (3) Employing and maintaining proper communication of organization operations.

Throughout history, wars and/or military conflicts have often been preceded by "a war of words." Many of these words were written in various newspapers, quoting the leading politicians and individuals of the day. Their words were used to "fan the flames" of or for war. According to a series of interesting articles found on www.pbs.org/wnet/mediamatters/303/words.html, less than half of the 2,120 newspaper founded in America between 1690 and 1820 survived for more than two years. But, some of these newspapers played an important role in America's Revolutionary War and the foundation of the United States.

America's first independent political newspaper, the New York *Weekly Journal,* was founded in 1733 by John Peter Zenger, who printed the controversial newspaper to challenge New York's equally-controversial governor, William Cosby. On November 17, 1734, Zenger was arrested and charged with seditious libel against Cosby. At Zenger's trial, his lawyer, Andrew Hamilton, convinced the jury that Zenger had a duty to "oppos[e] arbitrary power . . . by speaking and writing the truth." When Zenger was found innocent, the verdict in effect opened the doors of criticism against the British government by American journalists. Soon, many American newspapers were voicing their opinions against their British rulers, speaking out against Britain's Stamp Tax and the Townshend Acts. Ultimately, in April 1775, these "war of words" led to the firing of the first shots of the war at Lexington. In his patriotic newspaper, *Massachusetts SPY,* Isaiah Thomas painted the British army as soldiers who were ". . . seeming to thirst for BLOOD" and who started the war ". . . by firing on the small party in which they killed eight men on the spot and wounded several others before any guns were fired upon the troops by our men."

In our recent history, the United States and many other countries of the world have engaged in two wars with Iraq. On August 2, 1990, Iraq's leader Saddam Hussein ordered his army to invade his country's oil-rich neighbor, Kuwait. The United States and many other countries throughout the world began to condemned Iraq's actions. The "war of words" began. According to PBS's MediaMatters website, the media's initial response to Saddam Hussein's invasion to his oil-rich neighboring country focused on oil. The prestigious financial newspaper, *The Wall Street Journal,* wrote: "Mr. Hussein could easily take control of the entire Gulf oil region except Iran, which would give him a real prospect of controlling the world oil price." The newspaper also ran an editorial called "The Economic Threat," calling for an end to tax hikes as a means of stalling the rising oil prices. The day after the Kuwait invasion, President George Bush Sr. stated, "There is no place for this sort of naked aggression in today's world." This quote became the centerpiece of a *New York Times* editorial that praised Bush's initial reaction of barring trade with Iraq and freezing its assets and encouraged the rest of the world to stand behind his actions. In subsequent months, Bush and many countries of the world continued their verbal assault against Hussein. On January 17, 1991, five and a half months after Iraq's invasion of Kuwait, Bush, along with a coalition of military allies, launched a successful military campaign—"Operation Desert Storm"—to drive the Iraqi army back into Iraq and to free Kuwait. In less than two months, the mission had been accomplished.

"What," U ask yourself, "does divorce; political debates; the Enrons of the world; 18th century newspaper articles; and 'Oil Wars' have to do with me and the fact that I am stuck in a college speech class?" The answer is simple. These examples show us the importance of why we need to be effective communicators.

## YOUR DECLARATION OF INDEPENDENCE

As a professional educator and college speech instructor, I am about to write a statement that to some may sound arrogantly self-serving; but, I write it with a deep sense of conviction and humility and a keen sense of the awesome responsibility I have as a speech instructor. Here is the statement:

> *The speech communication class in which U are now enrolled will be the most important class you will ever take in college.*

> *"Whoa!," U say. "This guy is 'way out there.'"*

No; in reality, I believe I am on safe ground in this statement. No matter what academic course U choose to study; no matter what profession or job U choose to enter; no matter what direction your life will take, everything U do (or will do) involves (or will involve) communication. There is a simple, yet profound, statement in Wood's textbook that supports this

## Communication Philosophy 27

Photo courtesy of Photos.com

fact. She writes: "We can not not communicate." Whether we want to or not, we are always communicating a message—or **meaning**—to the world around us. One of the secrets of success is that words, thoughts and ideas are powerful. Those who learn to use words properly in written and oral presentations and learn to communicate effectively on a personal and professional level are highly sought by employers. After they are hired, they usually find themselves climbing corporate ladders more quickly than those who possess inferior communication skills.

Think about some individuals U consider as "successful." No matter how U may define "success," more than likely your choices possess better-than-average oral and written communication skills. They are individuals who can clearly articulate their ideas and feelings. They know their strengths and their weaknesses; and, they are on a constant quest to improve their communication skills.

Of course, in reality, your speech course will be what U make it. Everyday, we all make life-changing choices. Some college students choose to sit back and not to take advantage of the "wonderful opportunities" they have to learn from their teachers and their fellow-classmates. Don't be one of those students. Choose to learn and understand the importance that effective communication plays in your life. Immerse yourself in this knowledge. It will change your life—for the better. It can become your personal Declaration of Independence.

## IS THE "F" WORD GRIPPING U?

Don't let FEAR grip U! The number one reason that students tell me that they dread taking a speech class is FEAR! They are afraid of standing up in front of other people. They are afraid that they will "say stupid stuff." They are afraid that other students will not like the way they sound or look

## 28 Communication Odysseys

when they stand and talk. They are afraid that they don't know enough to talk about anything for five minutes. They are afraid that they will make a bad grade. The list of "they are afraid" statements could fill the rest of this chapter; but, U get the point. FEAR is gripping and controlling them. But, FEAR is a self-induced emotion. No outside entity can force FEAR upon anyone. We choose to embrace FEAR. We allow this emotion to overwhelm us. But, the good news—which was so eloquently stated by President Franklin D. Roosevelt in his first inaugural address on March 4, 1933—is that "We have nothing to fear, but fear itself." By following the tips on how to conquer your FEARS that U will find later in this book and by allowing your speech teacher to lead and guide U outside your "safety zone," U will begin to experience a freedom and confidence that U have never known.

So, where does this journey of learning to become an effective communicator begin? It begins with U.

## SO, WHO ARE U?

> *The two greatest quests of humanity are to know and to be known. The search for truth propels us on a journey of lifelong discovery, both inwardly and outwardly. At times, this search gently nudges us; at other times, it drags us out of the darkness toward the light of truth. It is when we finally come to bask in this light that we fully know and that we are fully known.*

Even though I have probably never met U, let me tell U some things about U of which I am at least 99.9 percent certain. First, U are a live, breathing human being. U have red blood pumping through your veins. U live on planet Earth. U breathe air. U have never walked on the moon. U eat food. U drink liquids. U can read, speak and understand English—at least to some degree. Your days are divided into 24-hour increments. Therefore, U have the same amount of time that everyone else has. U have some hidden abilities and talents of which U are unaware. U have FEARS.

U are not perfect. U see the world around U filtered through your eyes of your experience and knowledge. U are a intricate part of the world around U. Without U, the world would be a different place.

"Gee," U are thinking. "This guy knows me like a book." U are right. I know a lot about U; and, U know a lot about me. As human beings, we share numerous common, life-sustaining experiences. These common experiences are a few of the foundational building blocks of our lives. These blocks help to build the stories of our lives.

## EVERYONE HAS A STORY. WHAT'S YOURS?

One of my former jobs I had before I became a college instructor was working as a reporter at several different newspapers. One of the most elementary assignments for any newspaper reporter is to write obituaries. Writing obituaries may seem like a mundane task, especially in light of all the "exciting" news that can be covered. But, in reality, obituaries are some of the most widely read news items that are printed in newspapers.

I have written hundreds, perhaps thousands, of obituaries. The thing that struck me as unusual about writing them was that I was commonly asked by editors to condense the story of a person's life down to four or five paragraphs. Generally-speaking, in writing obituaries, I would try to find an unusual or outstanding accomplishment the person had achieved during his/her lifetime and include it in the obit. At times, I was asked by editors to write a full-length obituary/story about a well-known person who had died. Still, it felt odd to me to try to write the story of someone's life and limit my words and thoughts to a few column inches of a newspaper.

I know—U are thinking, "What does the fact that this guy wrote obituaries have to do with me and the fact that I am stuck in this college speech class?" I am glad U asked. I'll answer your question by asking U some thought-provoking questions: When U die (or pass from this life to another type of existence), how will your obituary read? In other words, what is your story? How do U live your daily life? What have U done in your life? What have U accomplished? Is there any real substance to your life? When other people are talking about U outside your presence, what do they say? How do they describe U? Are their descriptions accurate? Is what they say about U true?

### *How Do U Tell Your Story?*

"But, what do these personal questions have to do with speech communication," U ask. The answer is: everything. U see, everyone's life is a story, and we spend our lives telling, or communicating, that story. Think about it. When U are talking with your best friend, what do U talk about most

Photo courtesy of Photos.com

of the time? The answer is: U! U may listen with interest as your friend talks about something that is going on in their life; but, more than likely, when it is your time to talk in a conversation, U are going to respond to your friend by telling him/her your story as it relates to their story. Together, in conversation, U both are **seeking to find and share the common meaning of your lives.** Simply stated, that is the definition of **communication: finding and sharing common meaning.** So, how do U tell your story when U are talking with your best friend? How do U tell it when U are talking with an acquaintance or with someone whom U have just met. How do U tell your story in a small group setting or before a large audience? What do U share about yourself? What subjects or matters are U willing to discuss openly about yourself? What are your secrets that U do not share with anyone?

Another question is: Why? Why do U tell people the things that U tell them. Why is it okay for U in your mind to tell your "secrets" to some people but not tell others? When U do choose to tell your story, why do U tell it the way that U tell it? I'm asking U these questions to get U to think about the matters that U do and do not discuss with others. Also, it is important for U to understand that the way that U communicate is important.

## How Does Your Story Affect the Way U Communicate?

Everyone has our own personal story of our daily lives. We are constantly telling and sharing some form of that story with everyone we meet. Remember: we can not not communicate. Even if we do not speak to those around us, we are telling our story of how we view life at that moment. If U are reading these words while sitting in the presence of others, take a moment and look around the room. If U see two people having a conversation, watch them for a moment. Observe how they are sharing their stories with each other. Now, look around the room and find someone who is sitting alone. Watch that person for a moment. Now, compare the differences in the way the couple who are engrossed in conversation and the person who is sitting alone are sharing the stories of their daily lives. In other words, observe how and what these individuals are communicating. What does their **body language** or **kinesics** say about their story? Do they appear to be happy? Are they smiling or laughing? Or, do they appear to be angry or upset? Can U "read" their story as U sit quietly observing them?

When we communicate, we are sharing with others who we are as individuals—we are sharing our stories with them. Whether we are sitting alone quietly or standing before thousands, the way that we share our stories is as important as the words that we use to tell them. The question "Who Are U?" leads us to another deeply thought-provoking question that affects the stories of our lives and the way we tell those stories.

## WHY ARE U HERE?

### *Have U Ever Pondered?*

The word "ponder" is a word that we don't use very often in the English language. I believe the reason that we don't use it very often is because in our busy, 21st century, American lives, we don't do very much "pondering" anymore. In the *Webster's NewWorld Compact School and Office Dictionary,* the word "ponder" is defined as follows: "to think deeply (about); deliberate." According to this concise definition, when is the last time U pondered anything?

Most of the times, we are so busy trying to fulfill the daily demands of our lives that we rarely have much time to think, much less, ponder anything. Most activities, that we must do in order to meet our physical needs, demand that we spend all of our time and energy thinking about them. In my own personal and professional life, I can get so wrapped up in worthwhile activities that I find myself driving from one meeting or engagement to another. At the end of the day, I find that I am usually drained of most of my mental, emotional and physical resources. "Pondering" is not on my list of things to do.

Photo courtesy of Photos.com

Probably the greatest thought that has ever been pondered by humanity has been this question: Why Am I Here? This is definitely a profound question. An amazing thing happens when different individuals ponder this serious question. They all come up with varied answers. The answers may have some similarities; but, ultimately, the answers to this question will be different. The reason is because we answer the questions of life that are posed to us based upon what we believe; and, as you will read later in this chapter, we all believe different things.

## GREAT PHILOSOPHERS WHO PONDERED LIFE

Throughout history, great philosophers have pondered the great questions of life. Since I began my college teaching experience, I have found that most college students I have taught have heard of Aristotle, Plato and Socrates, three of the great Greek philosophers. But, although many of the students have heard the names of these men, they have never studied or learned anything about their teachings about the principles of life. In his book, *Basic Teachings of Great Philosophers*, author S. E. Frost examines of the teachings of 125 philosophers who have lived throughout history. It is a good, practical guide to gaining some basic knowledge concerning philosophers and their teachings.

## BACK TO U AND YOUR EXISTENCE

Once again, I "hear" U asking me a question: "So, what does all this stuff about philosophers and philosophy have to do with me and the fact that I am stuck here in this college speech class? How is all of this stuff going to make me a better communicator and speaker?" U said the magic word when U asked your question. The word: HERE.

Perhaps the speech communication course in which U have enrolled was a required class for your major. Maybe, U are one of those rare college students who freely chose to enroll in the class. Whatever's the case, the fact is that, at this moment, U are HERE. U are reading this sentence that I wrote several months, perhaps years, ago, as I anticipated this moment of connection with U. U will have to ponder and decide how U got HERE. It may be a long, painful, soul-searching process of discovery for U. But, the fact is that U are now HERE. So, I will ask U another thought-provoking question to ponder: Now That U Are Here, What Are U Going To Do?

This can be the dawning of a new day for U. If U allow yourself to do so, U can change. U can learn to be a better communicator. I've seen this change occur in the lives of many students, but, they had to be willing to take a risk—to step outside their comfort zone. They had to be willing to be stretched and pulled—to think beyond their normal way of thinking. In essence, they had to be willing to become pliable clay, in order to be molded into the vessel they were meant to become. Their change came through understanding that they needed to change. They began to understand that, to some degree, they had spent their lives just talking, rather than truly communicating. They let go of the FEAR they were gripping and began holding on to a new way of looking at and communicating with the world around them. U can become one of the students I have just described. All U have to do is BELIEVE.

## Say What?

All communication is rooted in what we believe about the present; the past; the future; ourselves; the billions of other people with whom we share planet Earth; and the existence or non-existence of God) or a Supreme Being or a Being Beyond the Dictates of the Natural World Order). These beliefs are the basis of how we view the world around us. The worldview—that is and is becoming uniquely ours—and no one else's—molds and shapes how we communicate with those with whom we come in contact. These beliefs are the foundational blocks with which we build our lives.

## What Do U Believe?

According to U.S. Census records, there are almost 6.5 billion people living on planet Earth on the date that I am writing this chapter. According to other world population data sources that I found on the Internet, on January 1, 1970, there were only 3.9 billion. This means that in less than 40 years, the Earth's population has almost doubled. This is an amazing figure. But, even more amazing than population numbers is the fact that every one of the people who are currently living on planet Earth have their own, unique set of beliefs and customs. They are all uniquely different. No two people on earth have duplicate identical sets of beliefs. People may share some common beliefs; but, they often vary in the details of their beliefs.

Photo courtesy of Photos.com

Human beings have many different beliefs. Some believe in God; others don't. Many Christians believe that Jesus Christ was and is God's Messiah; the Jewish faith does not accept Jesus as the Messiah. Hindus believe in many gods. Other religions taught and practiced throughout the world have their own unique set of beliefs. But, beliefs are not limited only to the divine realm. People believe many other things. To some, another person's beliefs may seem quite strange or unfamiliar. To others, those same beliefs would be commonly known and accepted. Some people believe in UFOs and that intelligent life exists beyond our world as we know it. Some believe in ghosts and the supernatural realm; others do not. Some say they believe only what they can see or experience with their five natural senses. Some people believe that death occurs, a person's life ceases to exist. Others believe in an afterlife. Some believe in heaven and hell; some believe just in heaven; still others do not believe in either heaven or hell. Some people believe man never walked on the moon. They believe that the televised jaunts on the moon by astronauts are staged events and are created in secret sound studios and broadcast throughout the world. I could spend my entire lifetime writing about what human beings believe or don't believe. But, that would not be as productive for me as asking U a few more thought-provoking questions. First, what do U believe? Second, why do U believe the things that U believe?

As an exercise, sit down with a few sheets of paper and write down all the things that U can think of that U believe. After U have made your list, take each item/subject on the list and write down why U believe the item/subject U have listed.

I hear your voice in my head again. "What the heck does what I believe have to do with the way I communicate?" I hear U asking. The answer is simple—EVERYTHING! As I have stated, our beliefs help us to form our worldview; and, our worldview becomes a part of the story about ourselves that we share with others. In other words, we are constantly communicating what we do believe and what we don't believe with others; and they are doing the same thing with us.

In your college speech course, U will be asked to stand before your classmates and share your story with them. U will be probably be asked to research controversial topics—topics U do not normally consider—and share what U believe about your assigned topic. This can be an enjoyable experience for U. Let go of your FEARS about your inadequacies of speaking before a group of people. We all have them. But, they can be overcome by preparation and practice.

Now, in my mind, I hear U asking me your last question concerning this chapter. "Why did U use "U" each time U referred to me when U were writing this chapter?" U ask. The answer is simple. I wanted U to understand that, even though I may not know U personally, U are important to me. I wanted to share with U a part of what I have learned and experienced. I wanted U to know that I believe that (capital) "U" are just as important as (capital) I am in the story of life. In a small way, our individual stories have now crossed paths. Both of our lives are now different. Because we have met (through the experience of U reading what I have written), our lives will never be the same. I encourage U to go out and share with the world around U what U have learned.

# Suggested Activities

NAME _____  DATE _____

## 4 U

1. Go to your favorite shopping mall and sit in the food court in a location where you can observe both those sitting in the food court and those who are walking by. Watch how the world around U is communicating with others. Write down your thoughts concerning the things that you see.

2. Begin to pay closer attention to the lecture presentations of your college teachers. Which teachers are getting through to U? Which teachers seem to be "lecturing" U rather than "communicating" with U? Study the speaking techniques of those teachers with whom U "connect."

## Vocabulary

Define these words:

1. Communication
2. Labels
3. Meaning
4. Kinesics
5. Philosophy
6. Beliefs

# Chapter 3
## Communication Models

In order to become effective communicators, we must first understand what communication is and how it occurs. Since the study of speech communication began, researchers have tried to explain the process of communication. To do this, scholars developed models to illustrate the steps and facets of the transmission of ideas. The models began rather simply but have evolved to more accurately capture the essence of interaction. The models we will focus on are models of dyads, or of two people interacting.

### LINEAR MODELS

Linear models were the first to be developed by researchers. They are the most basic, and therefore the least effective.

**LINEAR MODEL**

Sender ⟶ Receiver

In the above model, we see that the **sender** is the person who is communicating. The **arrow and line** represents the message being sent to the other individual, who is the **receiver.**

The shortcomings of this model may be obvious. First, the model shows communication as a linear event. One person speaks and the other person hears. However, communication is not linear. According to this model, if I am speaking to someone, the person to whom I am speaking is not communicating in any way. One of the principles of communication states that we cannot not communicate, it is always occurring. Therefore the model is not accurate.

Another problem is that it does not allow for any response to the original message. The linear models do not capture the dynamic nature of communication or the various factors that impact communication.

## INTERACTIVE MODELS

Interactive communication models add an important feature: **feedback.** Feedback is the response of the receiver to the original message that was sent.

---

**INTERACTIVE MODEL**

Sender                    Receiver

Feedback

---

Here we see that the receiver is giving feedback, or responding, to the sender's original message. While the Interactive Model is more accurate, it still portrays communication as linear. In this model, the sender sends the message, the receiver gets it, and then responds. Again, this implies only one person is communicating at a time. There is a model that is more effective.

## TRANSACTIONAL MODEL

The Transactional Model provides more specific details about the process of communication. There are many factors that influence our communication and transactional models incorporate these factors.

As you can see, the Transactional Model includes more components and is more detailed than those previously discussed. Here, the dynamic nature of communication is finally depicted. We can examine each component more closely.

### Sender/Receiver

Rather than portraying communication as linear, in this model each individual is both sending and receiving messages at the same time. For in-

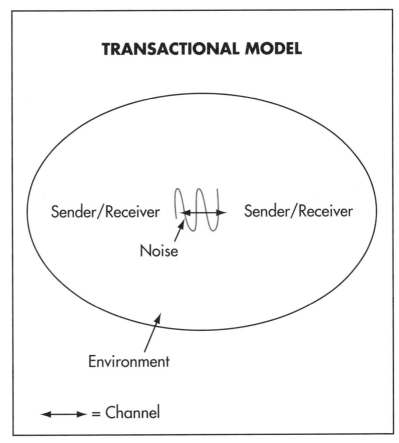

stance, if I am speaking to someone, I am sending messages and I am also receiving messages from him or her, perhaps in the form of nonverbal cues such as nodding or facial expressions. Similarly, while the other person is receiving my message, they are sending his or her own. This refers back to the idea that we are always communicating.

## Message

The message is simply the information that is being exchanged. It may be a greeting, providing directions, debating, showing affection, any type of information that can be exchanged.

## Channel

The channel is *how* the information is being exchanged. It is the manner in which we are communicating. The channel may be verbal, in which we are actually speaking to one another. It may also be nonverbal. Nonverbal communication occurs in many forms, from hand gestures to our tone of voice. Finally, the channel may be written communication.

## Noise

Noise is any interference with the message. Noise prevents us from receiving the message exactly as the sender intended. We are unable to escape noise, it is always present in some form. There are three types of noise that can create interference.

1. **External Noise**—Anything outside of the body. External noise may be loud noises that prevent us from hearing the message. It could also be something that distracts us in some way, such as other people talking around us. Have you have ever been talking on the phone and began watching TV instead of listening to the phone conversation? External noise may also be visual. If you are unable to read the chalkboard in a classroom because something is in the way, that is external noise.

2. **Internal Noise**—Anything inside the body. Internal noise occurs within us. There are two types of internal noise:

   a. **Psychological**—Psychological noise occurs in many forms. For example, even the most riveting class lecture sometimes fails to keep our attention. We may start daydreaming or creating a mental to-do list. Or perhaps we had a fight with a friend and find ourselves unable to concentrate. Our moods can be a type of psychological noise as well. If we are angry or in a bad mood, we may interpret a message more negatively than we do if we are happy.

   b. **Physiological**—Physiological noise results from the physical aspects of our bodies. There are many factors that can affect this type of noise as well. Fatigue, pain, hunger, illness, physical abilities, stress, and drugs, both legal and illegal, are all examples of physiological factors. If we have a headache or are overwhelmed with stress, it may prevent our ability to interpret messages accurately. We may even be unable to physically receive the messages.

   c. **Semantic**—Semantic noise occurs when we are unable to understand the symbols that are being used. Keep in mind that all communication, both verbal and nonverbal involves symbols. We may not know the symbols used or we may interpret them incorrectly. Trying to talk with someone who speaks a different language involves semantic noise. We literally don't know the words he or she is using.

## Environment

The environment is the context, or setting, of the communicative event. It includes where the communication is occurring, the specific aspects, other people, and the psychological climate. Are you in doors or out? Is the room large or small? Are other people present? If so, how many? What are the physical aspects of the environment? Is the climate relaxed? Tense? All of these factors affect the communication. Interaction will change based on how a room is set up, what color it is painted, the time of day, or how comfortable individuals feel.

Each of the components of the Transactional Model affects and is effected by the others. All must be taken into account when communicating in order for us to truly grasp what happens when we communicate and to apply this knowledge to improve our communication skills.

## Applying the Knowledge

Effective communicators are aware that they must take into account each of the components of the transactional communication model. Although this model focuses on a **dyad,** you can apply the information to various settings. If you are making a presentation to a classroom, for instance, evaluating these factors will help you achieve a more successful speech.

Using that scenario, let's perform an assessment of the communicative event. First, consider the message. What information are you trying to get across to your audience? What channel will be the most effective? If you will be discussing statistics, will the audience understand them best if you explain them verbally or would a graph they can read be helpful? How will your delivery impact the speech? Your nonverbal communication can add to or detract from your message. You will need to consider noise. How will you keep your audience's interest? Will semantic noise be a problem? You may need to take the time to define particular terms you will be using to ensure your audience understands your message. How will the environment affect the presentation? Where will you and your audience be situated? You will need to adjust your volume and the size of any visual aids, depending upon how large the room will be.

The process of communication is a complicated one. But once you learn to consider the various influences on our communication, you are on your way to becoming a more aware communicator. This awareness is the first step in becoming a more effective communicator.

## Psychology and Communication

Many students are familiar with Abraham Maslow's hierarchy of needs model created in the 1940s and 50s to explain human motivations and desires. Strongly tied to Fruedian thinking, and also behaviorist psychology, Maslow tried to account for human actions and motivations in an all encompassing chart that perhaps doesn't do justice to the complexity of human desires, but provides a clever and effective shorthand

## Abraham Maslow's Hierarchy of Needs and Communication Needs

6: Communication facilitates all needs

5: Growth self actualization full being

4: Esteem status achievement self worth

3: Belonging family relationships meaningful work

2: Safety protection limits and law

1: Basic needs: food, water, sex, shelter, air

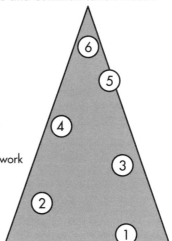

to understand why people do as they do, and perhaps more importantly, why they speak as they do. Probably 95 percent of the motivations underlying contemporary detective programs can be found here. At the most **basic level,** Maslow argues that people need the basic commodities of **food shelter and air** to survive. **Sex** is included in this stage because it is a primal physiological urge, a fact that our puritanical society would often like to overlook, but well, there it is.

Once we arrive at level one and can sustain ourselves temporarily, people require a sense of **protection and safety** from potential future harm. At the **second level,** the child that asks to be tucked in to bed at night sees the world as threatening and requires reassurance against harms. This **third level** is a level of **belonging,** that sense that individuals are a part of a larger collective and that they can be supported and accepted by a group of peers. This includes long term relationships such as marriage where people are willing and able to form lasting partnerships and unions. The **fourth stage** involves **personal worth** and work at a level that achieves a sense of well being and fulfillment. A person that is promoted, moved to a new position, or achieves trust, can feel better about who they are. Finally, at the **fifth stage,** we reach **self-actualization** or the fulfillment of self and potential abilities. Perhaps one becomes a concert pianist, a successful mother, a doctor, or sculpture. Whatever the personal goal that brings joy and fulfillment, the success at that level provides a sense of completeness to one's life and personal mission. Not to say that all of these levels are flat and static. Quite the contrary. Maslow saw these ideas as being transitory and what provided belonging and well being at one stage of life could prove unfulfilling later. At 20, a position with a meager paycheck may be sufficient for a young unskilled wage earner, but as the worker progresses that person will require more achievement, more belonging, more responsibility and more challenges to maintain a sense of well being. There have been many studies done of retired people, and one thing that is common is a sense that without work a sense of mission and internal motivation is often lost.

Finally, we have introduced a new level at the top of Maslow's pyramidal hierarchy. This is not to trump Maslow and to suggest that communication is more important than the other needs, merely to suggest that communication is the mainspring from which other needs are made known, engineered and eventually accomplished. In the end, needs must be communicated to others. Others must be engaged in their accomplishment and finally, others provide the fabric of society upon which our achievements and contributions are forged. Without communication to others, there can be no sense of needs having been met. Consider, President Bush, who has successfully been re-elected president in 2004. Whether or not as a citizen, you agree with Mr. Bush's agenda, one must respect that he has a vision and that he has successfully encouraged a large number of Americans to share his vision through crises of war, unemployment, high fuel prices, 911, and a rising deficit. He clearly obtains Maslow's high order of self-actualization fulfillment from his work, and his method of achieving his goals has largely been through his communication skills, something he has steadily improved upon during his term as president. This is not an ill-considered linkage and it speaks to importance of communication in meeting the Maslowian hierarchy of needs.

## POLITICAL COMMUNICATION MODELS

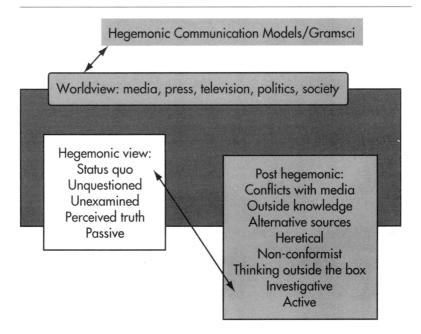

In the political communication model determined by **Antonio Gramsci,** society was thought to be determined by Marxist economic models. A **hegemony** or a **hegemonic concept** is an unchallenged prevailing social orthodoxy that is resistant to change because it is very rarely effectively questioned. In fact that society often hides such underlying issues so they are not questioned. Gramsci, an Italian, Marxist philosopher, argued that the economic system even pervades the social system and what becomes true in economic terms becomes accepted wisdom in social terms. For example, if it is thought that poverty is not due to unequal distribution of wealth but due to individual laziness, the society will adopt the idea that poverty stems from lazy behavior not the power of society that distributes capital poorly amongst potential competitors.

This may seem remote from communication but it is a central issue of **what to believe or what not to believe.** If you only hear one side of events constantly, it is likely you may be the victim of **hegemonic bias.** The secret to the success of such bias is that it can go **unchallenged and uncontested** by most people for a very long time. The fact that certain **assumptions are never questioned** or thought to be questioned makes it hard to overthrow them. Just some simple hegemonic prejudices that only recently have received scrutiny suggest how successful hegemonic ideas are at controlling thought. Why does the press concentrate on issues such as gay marriage or abortion when more pressing issues are unemployment, fair wages, or universal health care? Why are most airplane pilots male? Why are most nurses female? Why has there been little new job growth for men in the past 20 years and enormous job growth and opportunity for women? This is a wide range of issues and there is no one answer or in fact any easy answer to any of these issues, but hegemonic thinking presumes that **"this is the way things are and should be,"** and therefore change is harder to accomplish.

Some hegemonic ideas include the powerful idea that **Fascist Germany** during the reign of Hitler had the right and the moral duty to declare war on Europe and to assume dictatorial control of the continent. Germans rarely questioned this concept that seemed like madness to most of the world. In this country, following **911,** good reason bowed to fear and paranoia and the **United States launched an attack on Iraq** on the basis of what then CIA director George Tenet and then Secretary of State Colin Powell, later referred to as 'flawed intelligence.' The war that has cost 100,000 Iraqi lives, over 1600 American lives and perhaps 500 billion US tax dollars continues all due to mistaken intelligence that everyone including the president believed. The hegemonic idea underlying this attack was that Iraq had WMD and they were involved in the 911 attacks. No proof has ever been found of either claim.

However, more importantly in communication, **hegemonic issues control communication and behavior** in even more insidious ways. Hegemonic ideas control gender roles (boys as doctors, girls as nurses). They control ideas about economics. (Taxation is always bad. Tax breaks are always good.) They control norms of beauty, what Naomi Wolf calls "the beauty myth," that makes women spend billions a year to look beautiful and results in controls on women's behavior. They control religious notions. (Abortion and gay marriage should be central issues in our society? Religion should be involved in government decision making?) Commercials exploit hegemonic ideas about prosperity, hedonism, and good living. Programs like *Extreme Makeover* exploit the idea that no woman's body is perfect until its perfected by plastic surgery.

British university professor **Stuart Hall** has proposed a simple and effective way to argue with hegemonic ideas when you see unquestioned but seemingly wrong assumptions. He argues that citizens can **decode messages** in an **oppositional and contrary manner.** That is, if you are told that mostly men become doctors, most young talented women could argue with that notion to achieve social parity. If you are told that network programming is good and you find it dull and uninspired you could experiment with cable programming to determine if there is better programming available. If you find commercial radio stations stale and too similar to each other, you could seek out alternative internet or satellite stations for alternative listening. These are means of alternative decoding of the media to seek and discover messages outside the mainstream.

## MEDIA AND MODELS

### Powerful Effects/Models

The manner in which media impacts individuals has been hotly debated since media began to influence people. In the 19th century, the **penny press** made newspapers so widely available that for the first time, people had a flood of new information daily that previously had been unavailable to them. By the end the century, in 1900, the **telegraph** had linked the Eastern United States to the Western states, and events in Washington, DC, could be related to Washington state almost instantaneously. In 1800, the same message might have taken weeks or months to travel the harsh 3,000 miles across the country. Immediately, people began to theorize how the media might be impacting the minds of the population. Obviously since the media could influence so many people simultaneously, it was thought at first that their effect was broad, powerful and monolithic. This is the hypodermic needle or bullet effect. That is, like a hypodermic needle or bullet, the media could penetrate our defenses and strongly influence our behavior.

### Moderate Effects Theory/Model

This theory of media influence was followed by a period of moderate effects thinking. Here it was assumed the media might have some effect but

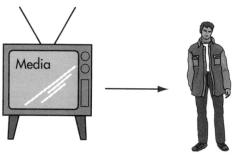

that effect was moderated by a variety of factors: exposure, societal setting, family influence, competing media, and personal mediation. It was assumed that people could think through what the media was trying to do to influence them and to some degree, an audience could successfully disagree with media messages and counteract such influence. An important study by **Hovland** in the 1940s brought this point out. Hovland was studying the impact of U.S. propaganda on American soldiers during WWII. It was assumed that since the soldiers worked for the government and the government could teach the soldiers what they should know about enemies such as Germany and Japan that soldiers would be highly susceptible to media influence. That is, the soldiers, according to the powerful effects model would hear information and accept it as truth, even if it was lying propaganda. Hovland discussed something very profound. First, the government could gain the soldiers' ears and eyes readily, and they could compel the soldiers to watch lots of pro-government media. This then, one would assume would cause soldiers to be easily indoctrinated. But Hovland found that in the responses of the soldiers there could be active and powerful resistance against simply swallowing messages at face value. The soldiers could mediate these messages, and think as they pleased while still watching and appearing to support whatever message the army gave them. This prompted Hovland and others to realize that media interactions were complex and that audiences could choose responses. The media may not have been as powerful as once thought. This research had a profound effect on groups that had wished to ban violence on television. If it was assumed that television alone prompted behavior, then it should be controlled, but if the communication landscape was more complicated and television could not control behavior, then perhaps it wasn't so important to tightly regulate it.

## Powerful Effects AGAIN!

Following a period in which the media was thought to compete with each other, and the effects of media were mediated by family, society, and social constraints, we have entered a new era that is media dominated and

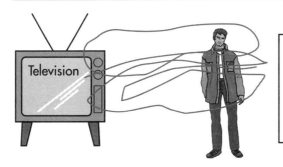

intensively pushing audiences into media interactions. The term **push media** was created around the year 2000 to describe the new media environment where new services and options would literally be pushed on audiences, and they would be given media choices. . . . but only prescribed media choices, not opt out choices. An example of this new push media is cell phones. A necessary device but now so compelling that text messaging, constant calls, and little quiet or disconnected time is tolerated. Calling plans promote more calling not less, and we spend time calling while shopping to discuss what we should be shopping to purchase. In one incident, I heard a cell phone caller speaking to another shopper in the same store to coordinate their shopping activities within the store. The cell phone has hooked Americans into dependence on the cell phone. Cable has hooked Americans into continually utilizing cable services for internet and cable television information. The long term effects of this new media model are uncertain, but at present it is thought the media can have broad power to **set agendas,** prime reactions, and condition responses to the environment. McCombs and Shaw in a 1972 study in North Carolina determined that the media could tell audiences what were important issues and audiences were likely to respond in concert with media choices. If the media tells you that gay marriage is a more important issue than wars in Iraq and Afghanistan, McCombs and Shaw would argue most people would support the media assumption of important issues. The functions of television in **priming** and **framing** are more specific. According to Iyengar at Stanford and other researchers, television can effectively prime our reaction to candidates and their validity in an election. A priming effect would be to determine if a candidate's war record is more important than their work in office. If the media decides to focus on war record, then people will make that the deciding factor in a candidate's race for office. If the media decide that current work is more important, they can prime that factor and bring it to audience attention. Framing is similar. Television can frame issues. In Michael Schudson's *Discovering the News,* he argues that bias has risen in recent years and is almost impossible to avoid. In fact he argues that news became obsessed with objective reporting, "precisely when the impossibility of overcoming subjectivity in presenting the news was widely accepted and . . . precisely because subjectivity had come to be regarded as inevitable."[28]

Finally, theorist and researcher, **George Gerbner** arrived at **cultivation theory** that said that the media can determine our world view and can cultivate a way of actually seeing the world. If by watching *Law and Order* five times a week, you begin to think that crime is a big problem that is because the media has induced that idea, cultivated that world view in you by showing repeated and continual criminal acts. You may wish to reject such notions but when the overwhelming media evidence suggests crime dominates American life (EVEN WHEN IT IS COMPLETELY UNSUBSTANTIATED AND WRONG) people will begin to see the world this way.

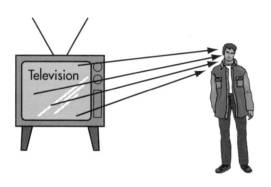

Powerful effects theory again
1975-Now
Subtle and powerful
Long term and unnoticed
Deep influence
Undetected but hegemonic
Unquestioned and unevaluated

## *Marshall McLuhan: Hot and Cool Media Models*

**Marshall McLuhan** was a theorist who hypothesized that media impacted the world in profound and often unrecognized ways. One of his models was regarding the subject of **hot and cool media.** Though his model doesn't directly relate to speaking, it does relate directly to how speech and communication events are presented to audiences and therefore how they receive such events and react to them. If McLuhan was right (and there have been some studies to confirm this since his theories arrived), media could have both a more profound and subtle effect than previously imagined, and a lesser effect than people think.

### Hot and Cool Media Theory

In a nutshell, McLuhan argued that all media could effect audiences in a variety of ways along a gradient of reactions. Those media that had a subtle, unpronounced but pervasive effect he termed cool media. Those media that had a direct, immediate and detectable effect were termed

## Hot Media Model

hot media. For example, for McLuhan, a hot media might be loud music in a dance club that gets a group of people up and dancing immediately. The music is loud, intense, and inspiring. It makes the audience members react almost involuntarily because it is so intense. The loudness, the percussiveness, the fact that it is unavoidable, that people came to the club to dance and listen all contribute to it being hot. It has a strong and compelling impact on people right away. Remember, this theory is not necessarily **media deterministic.** Media determinism suggests that the media can actually determine your behavior. Most people no longer believe that. That is, just because the media is there does not demand that you must dance. People aren't robots and people can CHOOSE not to dance. However, McLuhan would argue that when a stimulus is so intense, it is more difficult to reject its allure than if the media was merely a subtle sound deep in the background.

**Cool media** are the more subtle representations of media and therefore a bit harder to determine as effects. However, they do produce effects only such effects are more subtle and less easy to recognize or directly link to a particular effect. For example, a person might watch police shows on television for a number of years, and this might shape their attitudes about lawlessness and crime. If they see lots of crime portrayed (and certain types of people committing those crimes), they may begin to have prejudices about criminals, crime, and fears that could be termed unrealistic, but motivated by the subtle and continual influence of pervasive but cool media. Perhaps a better illustration of cool media at work would be the radio. It is often on in people's cars delivering commercial messages about buying cars, drugs, or certain personal items. Over time, the ignored radio messages could have a subtle effect on the audience. At the time you hear the commercial you may reject it or think that it does not influence you in any way. But years later after hearing one dealer's commercial message for years at a time, when you become ready to buy a car, that dealer's name (regardless of how you felt about their commercial) might remain in mind, and you may even visit that dealer simply out of familiarity. Thus, car dealers and other powerful sellers bomb the airwaves with constant and continual commercials hoping that this subtle effect will seep into the audience over time. If such an effect is successful, it would be an example of McLuhan's cool media effect.

**Cool Media Model**

# Chapter 4

## Communication and the Performance

In his song, "It Ain't Over 'til the Fat Lady Sings," legendary Nashville songwriter Danny Dill (who wrote the classic country songs "Detroit City" and "The Long Black Veil") wrote a clever couplet based upon the work of the great English playwright William Shakespeare. Shakespeare wrote:

> *All the world's a stage, and all the men and women merely players: they have their exits and their entrances; and one man in his time plays many parts, his acts being seven ages.*

In other chapters I have stated that we are constantly telling and re-telling the stories of our lives with others. In his song, Dill is saying the same thing; but, he refers to our "stories" as "the show." Think about the last theatrical production that U attended. What was the intent of the actors (Dill's "players") of that production? No matter how good or bad the production may have been in your mind, the "players" were doing their best to "perform" a story for U and your fellow audiences members. By using their voices; their understanding; their memories; their movements; their gestures; and their confidence or "presence," the actors were trying to tell a story. They were trying to communicate with U what the author or playwright of the "show" wanted to say—the show's message or **meaning.**

Whether delivering an informal speech before a speech class or speaking before a Toastmasters Club or making a formal address at a business meeting or political gathering, excellent communicators understand that performance is one of the keys that unlocks the hearts of listeners. They understand their role as players. They are there, in a sense, to entertain—"to act out our part" as the messenger. They also understand that they "can stick the script of play it by heart."

In this chapter, we will examine the "show business" aspect of speech-making—the glitz and glamour—the fun stuff. Hopefully, U will begin to understand the importance of your voice and how to use it to your advantage, not only in giving a speech, but, also, in your personal life. U will learn some basic stage movement techniques and effective gestures that are used by both great actors and great public speakers. Finally, U will learn that U have the power to "command" an audience—to evoke from them the response from them that U want them to make. This will be a fun chapter for U, because, as Ethel Merman use to sing in the famous musical "Annie Get Your Gun," "There's No Business Like Show Business."

## A STAGE IS A STAGE IS A STAGE

> *Oh, those nasty, articulate ancient Greeks and Romans!*

### *The Greeks*

The idea that great actors and great orators share common family roots is not a new one. Roman philosopher, orator and politician Marcus Tullius Cicero wrote *De Oratore*, a study of the art of public oratory, in 55 B.C. *De Oratore* and other writings by Cicero were translated in a work by J.S. Watson titled *Cicero on Oratory and Orators* published in 1876. Throughout his writing, Cicero points to the techniques and skills share by both the actor and the orator. In one passage, Cicero wrote:

> *". . . But in an orator, the acuteness of the logicians, the wisdom of the philosophers, the language almost of poetry, the memory of lawyers, the voice of tragedians, the gesture almost of the best actors, is required."*

In this writings, Cicero lauded his friend—the great Roman actor of his day—Roscius, (whom Cicero obviously admired very much) as a role model for those public speakers who were truly interested in effectively reaching their audiences. He wrote:

> *". . . To judge therefore of the accomplishments of the orator by comparison with this stage player [Roscius], do you not observe how everything is done by him unexceptionally; everything with the utmost grace; everything in such a way as is becoming, and as moves and delights all? He has accordingly long attained such distinction, that in whatever pursuit a man excels, he is called Roscius in his art."*

As these passages of Cicero show, there are skills that are common in the repertoire of the trained actor that can be useful to the student—as well as the professional—orator. When looking at the history of speech, we often find names that are known figures in the history of theatre. Let's look at some figures of the ancient Western civilization who were influenced both the worlds of theatre and oratory.

The history of theatre and acting is almost as old as mankind itself. In most early civilizations, the component elements of acting and theatre—recitation, song and mimetic dance—existed. In one of the earliest forms of theatrical pageantry that dates to around 4000 B.C., the Egyptians probably staged dramatic performances based upon their religious traditions in which actor-priests combined dramatic action and religious celebration while worshipping the memory of the dead.

But, the roots of Western theatre are deeply planted in the soils of ancient Greece, where during the sixth century B.C., the first significant steps toward dramatic impersonation were taken. Thespis, who is generally regarded as the first actor, introduced this new technique of dramatic impersonation to the Greeks in the first half of the sixth century. (It is from Thespis' name that we derive our modern-day term for actors—thespians). At first, Thespis, who functioned as both dramatist and actor, was condemned when he brought his new technique to Athens around 560 B.C. Solon, an Athenian lawgiver, labeled Thespis' impersonations as dangerous deceptions. But, by 535 B.C., attitudes toward this "deceptive" art had softened, and the Greek tyrant Pisistratus introduced competitive performances for actors at the Dionysian festival in Athens. In honor of his contributions to the art, Thespis was crowned as the first victor at the festival. Each spring thereafter, at the City Dionysia—Athens' great religious festival—actors performed tragedies in honor of Dionysus, the goddess of wine and fertility.

As these contests continued and developed and became more elaborate, the art of acting and the status of actors grew. The dramatists and actors who participated in City Dionysia were regarded as some of Athens' most highly honored citizens. In the fourth century B.C., an actors' guild was established to preserve the civil and religious rights of actors. The guild helped its artists get privileges to travel during times of strife and exemption from military duty.

In the earliest Greek tragedies, one actor—usually the poet of the tragedy—would impersonate several characters while wearing different masks. The leading actor-poet and two other actors were aided by a chorus and its leader. This was the manner in which Thespis probably performed.

During the fifth century B.C., the poets was often the dramatist, stage manager and actor of theatrical performance. They chose other actors, who frequently became associated with their plays. For example, both Aeschylus and Sophocles followed Thespis in the actor-poet tradition. These actor-poets trained the chorus. Therefore, innovations in declamation and gestures are largely attributed to their genius.

Slowly, as actors gained prominence and skill, the state placed the actors with competing dramatists to prevent domination of drama competitions. During the fourth century B.C., actors began to replace the poets in importance, due to the diminishment of the literary creativity in tragedies. During this century, ancient Greek audiences were moved by the dramatic skills of the country's top tragic actors, including Aristodemus, Neoptolemus, Theodorus, Thettalus, Polus, and Athenodorus. As some of the actors of the 21st century are, some of those early Greek thespians were egomaniacs that made self-serving demands. For example, according to his demands, no other character was allowed to precede Theodorus on stage. This type of behavior was not accepted in the eyes of some of Greece's leading thinkers. The great Greek philosopher, Plato, who lived from 429 B.C. to 347 B.C., condemned the art of pantomime and poets in general. In his ideal republic, these people would be driven out of the country. About 2,000 years later during the Renaissance period, opponents of theatric performances frequently cited Plato to argue against the theatre and actors.

Another great Greek philosopher, Aristotle, who was Plato's student, was born in Stagira in 384 B.C. As a schoolmaster in Athens and as tutor to great conqueror, Alexander the Great, Aristotle produced volumes of writings on metaphysics, logics and politics, as well as studies on rhetoric and poetry. His writings are some of the world's most valuable sources on the Greek drama of the fourth and fifth centuries B.C. From his writings, *The Rhetoric*—which has been considered by most scholars as the "bible" of public speaking for more than 2,000 years—Aristotle asserted that the methods of delivery used by actors, poets and orators were basically the same, and he indicates some of those methods. In his work titled *Poetics*, which is the earliest known extant writings on dramatic theory, Aristotle charted the historical roots of drama in Greece. He described the number of players used in Greek performances and some of the qualities of actors and acting. In *Poetics*, he wrote:

> "... In composing, the poet should even, as much as possible, be an actor; for by natural sympathy, they are most persuasive and affecting who are under the influence of actual passion. We share the agitation of those who appear to be truly agitated—the anger of those who appear to be truly angry."

## *The Romans*

Today, Roma (Rome) is a bustling, modern-day metropolitan city that exudes life and energy. Having married a "Roman," I have had several opportunities to travel to this wonderful city and have spent more time there than an average tourist. To me, the really amazing aspect of the city is that often many of its modern buildings stand next to structures or monuments that are thousands of years old. Probably the best-known ancient day structure still standing in Rome today is the Colosseo (Coliseum). Although time has eroded its soaring walls, it is easy to imagine how impressive it must have looked to first century Romans. Even during that time, it represented all that was good—and bad—in the Roman Empire. On the good side of the equation, it was a marvelous representation of the Romans' abilities as architects. The basic structure of the Colosseo has stood intact for about 2,000 years. Unfortunately, on the negative side,

this was the place where, through its many years of activity, thousands of people were killed for sport and for their religious beliefs as thousands of bloodthirsty spectators cheered wildly.

On one of my tours of the Colosseo, I was able to stand for a long period of time and study the stadium's floor. It now stands uncovered and one can see the walls over which, in its heyday, the flooring was placed. The rows of walls were used to separate and house prisoners; vicious animals; and the gladiators or fighters. When the flooring was placed on top of the walls, it could be sealed and filled with water. Often, sea battles, featuring the real-life deaths of its participants, were recreated. Compared to these dramatic spectacles, the translated Greek tragedies and comedies of the ancient Roman theatre probably seemed like tamed, toothless tigers to Roman audiences.

Both acting and drama of the ancient Roman world were based upon the works of the Greeks. Livius Andronicus, a Greek captive in Rome, first introduced translated Greek plays to Roman audience in 240 B.C. Later, Roman comic writers, Terence and Plautues, as well as tragedy writers Pacuvius, Naevius Seneca and Ennius, all adopted or modified Greek subject matter or dramatic forms to tell Roman ideas and stories.

At first, Roman dramas were presented on festival days in temporary wooden theatres and on temporary stages that were erected in public places. As the number of festival days increased, permanent theatres were erected. Three magnificent theatres were built in Rome. Pompey built the first theatre in 55 B.C. Cornelius Balbus erected the second major theatre in Rome in 13 B.C. The third major Roman theatre was built by the Augustus the same year. These three buildings were the only permanent theatres in Rome. They were huge, sumptuously adorned structures and seated as many as 40,000 people. Joined together by exterior walls, a semi-circular orchestra and auditorium, a stage and decorated scene house formed an architectural unity. It was upon these stages that the adapted Greek plays were presented. However, the restrained nature of

Greek drama did not appeal to the Romans, who favored spectacular displays, such as the Colosseo's "sea battles." Although Roman plays were given on the occasion of various political, religious and military holidays—they did not have the ritual significance of the Greek contest. Often, dramatic performances were forced to share the stage with gladiatorial shows and chariot races, which were far more popular than the plays.

Most Roman actors were slaves and did not enjoy the lofty status that Greek actors had once enjoyed. As slaves, they had no religious or legal rights. Managers or masters were placed in charge of the training of these acting troupes of slave-actors. As slaves, they were treated according to the dictates of their masters. One such example is found in the epilogue of Plautus' *The Caskets*. In describing the rewards that a Roman actor could expect to receive for his performance, Plautus wrote: ". . . the actor who has made mistakes will get a beating, the one who hasn't will get a drink."

Aesop and Roscius, two of the most renowned actors of ancient Rome, lived in the first century B.C. Roscius became so wealthy and a man of such great distinction that he was freed from slavery. He became an acting instructor and became so renowned for his teaching ability that he was sought out by lesser actors-slaves for protection and training. Aesop was known for his emotional fire and tragic impersonations. During one of his performances, the Greek-born actor became so emotionally involved with his part that he killed another actor-slave.

For 20 years, Spanish-born Marcus Fabius Quintillian—who lived from 35 to 95 A.D.—was the head of the leading school of oratory in Rome and was an outstanding instructor in oratory and eloquence. Vespasian, the Roman Emperor, created a chair of oratory for him. After retiring from his teaching career, Quintillian wrote his great work, *Institutio Oratoria*, which outlined the necessary attributes and training of an accomplished public speaker. His instructions on the gestures and voice for the accomplished public speaker were probably based on observations of the Roman actors of his day. He did recognize acting and oration as different, separate arts; however, his writings have been used extensively in the education of actors. In 1913, Rev. John Selby Watson translated Quintillian's work. In *Institutes of Oratory*, the Roman teacher wrote that oratory students would do well to learn and employ the skills of actors; however, they should avoid the actor-slave's lifestyle:

> "Some time is also to be devoted to the actor, but only so far as the future orator requires the art of delivery; for I do not wish the boy, who I educate for this pursuit, either to be broken to the shrillness of a woman's voice, or the repeat the tremulous tones of an old man's. Neither let him imitate the vices of the drunkard, nor adapt himself to the baseness of the slave, nor let him display the feelings of love, or avarice, or fear; acquirements which are not at all necessary to the

*orator, and which corrupt the mind, especially while it is yet tender and uninformed in early youth; for frequent imitation settles into habit."*

## STARS OF THE STAGE AND SCREEN WHO FOLLOWED THOSE NASTY, ARTICULATE ANCIENT GREEKS AND ROMANS

Since the dramatic early days of Greek and Roman "stardom," the actor and his environment have dramatically changed. By the fifth and sixth centuries A.D., due to a decaying Roman civilization, the impact of conquering German forces, and, later, the stiff opposition of the Roman Catholic Church, acting in formal comedies and tragedies had become a lost art form. Thus, during the Dark Ages or the Middle Ages, there are very few recorded documents of theatrical activity. This does not mean theatrical activity was not happening. Acting knowledge and traditions were transformed into various other forms of entertainment, primarily music and mimes.

Ironically, the Church's opposition mellowed during the Middle Ages and the Church used actors' interpretations and enactments of biblical passages to develop liturgical drama. As these dramatizations grew, they eventually were moved from a church's choir space to the church's porch. In the 15th century, the live pageantry of the biblical stories were abandoned for another form of dramatic religious teaching known as morality plays. These dramatic sermon-plays depicted characters caught in a struggle between evil and good. These morality plays were influenced by humanists of the Renaissance period and represent a transitional state between religious drama and national secular drama.

During the Elizabethan Period in the 16th and 17th centuries A.D., William Shakespeare's plays dominated the theatrical landscape of England. Little is known about the acting styles employed by Shakespeare's company. Two Elizabethan "tragic" actors gained prominence during the era—Edward Alleyn and Richard Burbage. In praising the abilities of English actors, playwright Thomas Nashe gave Alleyn special recognition. He wrote: "Not Roscius, nor Aesop, those

Photo courtesy of Library of Congress

admired tragedians that have lived ever since before Christ was born, could ever perform more in action than famous Ned Alleyn."

Between the Elizabethan Period and the 21st century, millions of professional and amateur actors and actresses have participated in countless productions throughout the world. Since his day, the comedies and tragedies of Shakespeare have been translated, produced and performed in some form in most cultures throughout the world. Musical theatre—a wedding of musical performance interspersed with the acting of dialogue to tell a story—became a popular art form in the 20th century.

In the United States and throughout other countries of the world during the 20th century, live musical performances began to compete with and eventually dominated the landscape of theatrical stages and venues. Superb opera artists, such as Enrico Caruso, filled the theatres of New York and throughout the world during the early 1900s. But, it was not until his music was broadcast on live radio broadcasts that his fame and notoriety spread to the common man. Later in the century, on November 28, 1925, WSM Radio's George D. Hay, who labeled himself as "The Solemn Old Judge," kicked off a live radio program of fiddle music by renowned 80-year-old fiddler "Uncle" Jimmy Thompson, by introducing it as "The Grand Ole Opry." Thus, the longest-running live radio program in the world was born. The Opry and WSM Radio would help to birth and facilitate the growth of the Nashville music industry and country music as an art form.

With the inventions of recording equipment—which provided a way to produce a musical product—and the coming of age of radio—which served as a medium to promote the musical product—the touring country music artists became an even more pliable trade. The laws of supply and demand came into force. The public heard artists on radio (supply). The public would then request (demand) that these artists come to their area, so that they could experience the artist's music in a live performance. At the performances, the artists would sell recordings, photos and any other souvenir items they thought the public would buy. Thus, a new industry was born—the music industry. Artists from other genres of music, including jazz; pop; rock; soul; as well as gospel music, began to travel throughout the world, seeking venues and audiences where they share and sell their music. As has been stated, these performers and their performances began to compete for the public's entertainment dollars, and live theatrical productions, because of their costs and time factors, began to wane.

Live theatrical performances also were dramatically affected by the coming of age of motion pictures and television during the early 20th century. The number of live theatres and live theatrical performances has diminished, particularly in the Western world where these technological wonders are readily available. However, in parts of Asia and Africa and other Third World countries where—in some places—availability of electricity and electrical supplies are still limited—live theatrical performance is still a very popular form of entertainment for the masses.

# Communication and the Performance

In the 20th century, motion pictures and television gave birth to a new entity in the entertainment field—the Hollywood star. Throughout the years, thousands of actors and actresses have become wealthy and have reached legendary status because of their acting work in films and television. A list of the top twenty actors in the history of film would vary according to the critics one might ask. Some of the leading actors and actresses who were recognized for their excellent work in films and television include; Sir Lawrence Olivier, Gregory Peck, Marlon Brando, Jimmy Stewart, John Wayne, Vivian Leigh, Clark Gable, Katherine Hepburn, George C. Scott, James Dean, and many other legendary figures.

## COMING BACK TO U

"So," I hear U asking. "What does all this stuff about Greek and Roman actors; the "Dark Ages"; Shakespearean actors; famous opera singers; the stars of the Grand Ole Opry; and dead Hollywood actors and actresses have to do with me and the fact that I am stuck in a college speech class?" I'm glad U asked. All of these individuals possessed the same tools that U possess and that U are being asked to use in delivering a speech.

### They Had a Voice and Knew How to Use It

Probably the single-most important tool of an excellent public speaker is his/her voice. Most people in the world today have a voice; but, very few people know how to properly use their voices when they are speaking in public—or for that matter—in private. As great professional actors and singers know, their voice is their "bread and butter" in helping them make a living. Without their voice, actors can not speak the dialogue of the stories they tell. Unless their part called for them to remain silent throughout an entire production, they would be useless to a director. They simply could not do the required job. Without their voice, singers can not interpret the music of the songwriter. Every professional singer knows the music business axiom: "If you don't sing, you don't get paid." Therefore, whether performing night after night at rambunctious, live shows or recording in a sedate studio setting, a singer knows that he/she has to take care of and protect their voice.

Aristotle understood the major importance of the voice and instructed public speakers how to use their voices correctly. In his manual on effective oratory, *The Rhetoric,* Aristotle wrote:

> ". . . A third would be the proper method of delivery; that is a thing that affects the success of a speech greatly; but hitherto the subject has been neglected. Indeed, it was long before it found a way into the arts of tragic drama and epic recitation; at first poets acted their tragedies themselves. It is

*plain that delivery has just as much to do with oratory as with poetry . . . It is, essentially, a matter of the right management of the voice to express the various emotions—of speaking loudly, softly, or between the two; of high, low or intermediate pitch; of the various rhythms that suit various subjects. These are the three things—volume of sound, modulation of pitch and rhythm—that a speaker bears in mind. . . . When the principles of delivery have been worked out, they will produce the same effect as on the stage. But only very slight attempts to deal with them have been made and by a few people, as by Thrasymachus in this* **Appeals to Pity.** *Dramatic ability is a natural gift, and can hardly be taught. The principles of good diction can be so taught, and therefore we have men of ability in this direction too, who win prizes in their turn . . ."*

After hearing themselves speak on a recording or television program, I have heard numerous individuals comment: "I don't like the way I sound," or "I don't like my voice." "How can a person improve the sound—or tone—of their voice?" U ask. I'm glad U ask. Let me offer U some simple tips. In the *February, 2003—Phone Communication Skills Newsletter,* Judith Filek, who is President of her company called Impact Communications, Inc., Ms. Filek wrote an articled titled "How To Improve Your Telephone Voice." The guidelines she offered in this article were written for people who make their living by speaking on the telephone. These guidelines, along with some acting techniques I learned as an undergraduate theatre major at the University of Southern Mississippi, can also be used to help the public speaker to correctly use his/her voice.

1. **Breathe properly from the diaphragm.** To check your breathing pattern, place one hand on your diaphragm and one hand on your chest and then take a deep breath. If you do not feel your diaphragm moving, your breathing is shallow. Improper breathing will cause your voice to sound monotone or "tinny." Take frequent pauses as you speak to allow you to breathe properly. This will dramatically improve the richness and resonance of your voice. Your articulation and enunciation will become clearer, and non-words like "ah" or "um" will no longer be as prominent in your speaking vocabulary. Most importantly, the pauses will give U time to think about what U are going to say before U say it.

2. **Pay attention to your posture.** If U are speaking while U are seated, make sure that your feet are flat on the floor under your chair. Do not fold your arms across your chest if U are sitting. This will hamper your breathing. If U are standing and presenting a speech, make sure your feet are planted squarely beneath U—about your shoulder's width apart. Do not cross

your feet. Do not shift your weight to and stand on one leg. If U are nervous about what to do with your hands, place them palms down on the podium until U begin to feel comfortable in making your speech.

3. **Use gestures.** When U are talking with your best friend, U use gestures. Think of your audience as your best friend. How do U normally talk when U are talking with your best friend? U gesture. It is the natural thing to do. In making a speech, U want to communicate as naturally as possible. Do not use wild, un-natural gestures, unless there is a specific reason to do so. Even then, be careful, because if it is not obvious to an audience what U are doing and they do not understand why U are doing what U are doing, it will cause confusion for them, and U will lose their attention. The goal is to keep their attention.

4. **Walk around a bit, using the podium as your command station.** After U have learnt to keep your feet planted firmly on the floor, and U begin to speak with confidence, do something daring! Move around a little bit. If U move to the left side, step out with your left foot. If U move to the right, step out with your right foot. When U are walking, don't "step across your body." In other words, walk naturally. Use your movement to help U make the points in your speech. Pause and look around the audience. This will give U time to collect your thoughts; and, more importantly, it will give your audience the time to collect their thoughts, also. The goal is to communicate the thought, idea or point that U are trying to make. Take charge of your audience. Command their attention. U have something important to tell them. Tell them with authority and confidence, and they will believe U.

5. **Smile!** Believe it or not, the sound of your voice is warmer when a person smiles. Also, an audience will be more attentive to a person who smiles, because smiling causes a person to be more relaxed. The more relaxed and in control a person is, the more that an audience will believe them. Use humor. People love to laugh, and there is always something to laugh about; so, find that something.

6. **Don't stand in front of a group and read your speech to them.** I often have my speech classes to repeat these words after me: "This is not a reading class." If you stand before a group and read a manuscript, your audience will become bored very quickly. Know your subject. Use an outline or note cards to keep your thoughts on track. It is okay to read a lengthy quote; but, make sure U have practiced reading it before U present your speech. Make sure U know how to pronounce all the difficult words within a quote.

7. **Remember this axiom: People hear what they see.** This may seem strange to U; but not only do people hear with their ears, they also "hear" with their eyes. If U are giving a speech about how wonderful life is, but U are wearing a frown on your face, guess what your audience is hearing? They are going to believe the story that is written on your face. If U are unprepared when U stand before a group, U don't have to tell them; they will know it. They will "hear" it before U have a chance to apologize for being unprepared. But, if U are prepared, relaxed and confident, your audience will "hear" and believe U the moment U approach the podium. They will accept U and respect U.

8. **Start drinking—lots of water.** This will help to moisten your vocal chords. Don't drink caffeinated drinks before your speech. These drinks tend to dry out your vocal chords. It is good to keep your vocal chords as moist as possible. Avoid drinking milk or eating cheese products before your speech. These products cause mucus to form in the throat.

9. The most important thing to do when U are presenting a speech is to have fun with your audience. If you have fun with them, they will have fun with U—and U will be on your way to becoming an even more effective communicator.

In closing, the arts of acting and oratory both have roots planted firmly in the idea of communicating a thought or primary truth. Whether we are acting or speaking before a small group or a large audience, our goal is communicate the message that is important to us. By understanding the importance of the tools we have with which we communicate, we will begin to use them more effectively. U have been blessed with a voice and a mind for understanding. My challenge to U is to go forth and use them properly and become a more effective communicator.

## REFERENCES

*Communication Journeys* . . . Stuart Lenig. Kendall Hunt Publishing Co.

"How To Improve Your Telephone Voice." Judith Filek, President of Impact Communications, Inc. Feb. 2003 Phone Communication Skills Newsletter www.impactcommunicationsinc.com

*Actors On Acting*, Toby Cole and Helen Krich Chinoy. Crown Publishers, New York; fourth edition

www.opry.com

# Chapter 5

## Communication and Research

There are several steps involved in the process of writing a speech. As you begin, research will be one of the first steps. As you do, it is important to prepare, be aware of the types of sources, and to find reliable sources to employ. You will also need to conduct audience analysis, include support for your ideas, and work on the delivery of your speech.

## GETTING STARTED

### Select a Topic

Of course the first step in writing a speech is to select a topic. As you decide on your topic, consider first the type of speech you will be delivering. Different topics will be appropriate for different types of speeches. Will you be giving an informative speech or trying to persuade your audience? This will impact the type of topic you will need. Next, select a topic in which you are interested. Since you will be conducting research, it is much more motivating to do so when you want to learn more about the topic. Your interest is also vital when delivering your speech. It will be communicated to your audience through your words and nonverbal communication.

Finally, consider what you know. It is much easier to research and speak on a topic with which you are familiar. Your knowledge provides a starting point when researching. If you are unfamiliar with your topic, it can be difficult to know where to begin working on your speech.

### Develop a Specific Purpose

As you prepare your speech, consider your general purpose. This will usually be either to inform or persuade the audience about your topic. Developing this idea more will aid you as you research. A specific purpose states explicitly what idea(s) you want your audience to receive. For instance, a specific purpose may be: To persuade my audience that the death penalty is unfairly administered. From this point, I can develop a rough outline and plan my main points. This will help you focus your speech. Once you develop the specific purpose, write it down. As you research, you can often become overwhelmed by the amount of information you uncover. It is easy to become confused about what to include and what to omit. I may find a great article arguing that the death penalty is cruel and unusual punishment. Do I include this? I can return to my specific purpose and re-focus. I want to discuss the unfair administration of the death penalty. The article I found would probably not fit into the scope of my speech.

## *Get Organized*

Research can be messy. You often end up with tons of pieces of paper and vague recollections of what information you found where. It helps to start with a system from the beginning to keep you organized as you work. One method is using note cards. As you read through your sources and find valuable information, write it on a note card. On each card, include one specific piece of data, the source, and page number if applicable. If using an internet source, include the address. After you have completed your research, you will have a stack of note cards with all of your information. You can then organize the cards into your main points according to the information of the card. Another method is to use multi-colored sticky notes. Apply a main point to each color. As you find information, use the appropriately colored sticky note. As you begin to write your speech, you will be able to find all the information for each main point by finding the corresponding colors. These are only two possible methods, you may find another that works for you. Starting with a system will help you as you move through the stages of speech-writing.

## *Types of Sources*

There are four different types of sources you can use when researching your topic. Each type has positive and negative aspects. Consider using each type of source when conducting your research. This can help guarantee you will find the most accurate information.

### Internet

The internet can be an invaluable research tool. You are able to find a large amount of information quite easily. There are multiple search engines you can use to conduct a key word search. If you are unable to find good information with one, you can try another. There are also various types of information you can find online. There are organizational or government web sites, published research,

| Popular Search Engines | |
|---|---|
| Google | AltaVista |
| Ask Jeeves | Yahoo |
| Metacrawler | Dogpile |
| Webcrawler | Alltheweb |
| AOL | Hotbot |
| Teoma | Lycos |
| Looksmart | MSN |

or news resources available. However, some problems with internet research exists. Keep in mind that not all internet sites are up to date. There are also many personal web pages that may include personal opinions as opposed to accurate, objective information. It is necessary to scrutinize your sources to ensure you are finding reliable information.

### Text Sources

Text sources include books, journals and encyclopedias. Journals are different from magazines in that they are usually focused on a specific area of study and will publish the original research that is often summarized in magazines. The benefit of text sources is that they usually provide more in-depth information. Text sources will often result in more data you can use in your speeches. You will still need to ensure sources are current and unbiased. It is possible to search for these sources through the library catalog search engine and e-books. Databases are also available that provide access to hundreds of journals.

### Media Sources

Media sources include a variety of types. Newspapers, magazines, television, radio and movies are all considered media sources. Pamphlets and small publications also fall into this category. If your topic is an issue that is one that is popular or commonly discussed, you will often be able to find a multitude of media sources. You can often find the most up to date, detailed information through these sources. Library databases include millions of full-text articles and various radio and television transcripts.

### Interviews

Interviews are a great way to receive specific information geared toward your topic. Interviews should be conducted with someone who is an expert in a field related to your topic in order to get the best data. Interviews can be conducted in person, over the phone, or online. You will be able to develop questions directly addressing the areas on which you want to focus. There are some specific steps you should take in order to make the most from your interview.

1. **Schedule the interview.** After you have found an expert to interview, you will need to set an appointment. When you do, inform the interviewee of your topic and the type of information you would like. This allows him or her to prepare for the interview and gather the necessary data. You are more likely to have a productive interview when you schedule it beforehand than when you drop in or call on someone with no warning. If you plan to conduct your interview online, be sure you allow plenty of time for the person to respond and realize you have less control in that situation. The other person may or may not respond or do so in time for your speech.

2. **Research.** You should have begun your research before you conduct the interview. You should know your topic and the areas on which you would like to focus before you speak with the

interviewee. Otherwise, you may be unprepared and unable to ask for the information you need.

3. **Prepare questions.** One of the most common mistakes that is made when interviewing is the failure to prepare a list of questions before conducting the interview. There is often the perception that you can sit down and the interviewee will simply give you the information you need. By developing a list of questions before you speak, you will be prepared to direct the interview. This will allow you to focus on specific information for which you are looking. Usually, five good questions will suffice. You may omit or add questions in the course of speaking with your interviewee, but you will at least be prepared going in.

4. **Conduct the interview.** As you speak, you will need a way to record the information. You may wish to use a digital recorder. This will allow you to focus on listening without having to take notes and you will be able to review the interview as needed. If you plan to use a recorder, always ask permission and be prepared to take notes if your interviewee prefers not to be taped. If you must rely on note taking, you will not be able to record everything that is said and you will most likely be unable to get a direct quote. Write down only the main points, highlight, and perhaps some specific pieces of data.

5. **Review.** As soon as possible after the interview, review your notes. You will be able to fill out the details and include the ideas on which you would like to expand or do further research. If you wait, the chances are increased that you will forget the meaning of the notes you have taken.

6. **Thank your interviewee.** Soon after you conduct the interview, send a thank you note. Your interviewee has taken the time to speak with you and it is common courtesy to thank them for their time and assistance.

## *Ensuring Reliability*

As you conduct your research, you must consider the reliability of the sources you will be using. This not only ensures you will have accurate information, but it will increase your credibility with your audience as well. There are three factors to check for reliability.

1. **Recency.** Your sources need to be recent. The more current your research, the more likely it is to be reliable. As cultures, politics and events change, information can become obsolete or inaccurate. The importance of this factor may vary with your topic, but search for the most recent information you can find. If a source is older, search for more current data to support that source.

2. **Bias.** Bias occurs when a source takes one side of an issue. Usually, the information contained within that source will be slanted to support that viewpoint. Biased sources may not include accurate data and will not appear to be credible to your audience. If I am speaking against gun control and cite statistics from the NRA, it will not persuade the audience in the way that information from government statistics will.
3. **Accuracy.** Checking accuracy ensures that the information you are using is correct. Facts and statistics can be shaped to support a source's viewpoint. Even an unbiased source can have inaccurate data. The best way to check for accuracy is to double-check your information and employ different types of sources.

## Citing Sources

It is important that you give credit to your sources as you deliver your speech. There are two reasons citing sources is necessary. First, in doing so, you will avoid plagiarism. Plagiarism is using someone else's words or ideas without giving them credit. Next, when you have reliable sources and state them in your speech, it will help improve your credibility with your audience. Citing sources informs your audience that you have conducted research, are knowledgeable on your topic, and have credible sources that support your ideas.

To cite your sources in your speech, you should include each source as you discuss the idea you received from that source. If you state a person's name, you should include a title or provide some information explaining why that person is a reliable source. You will also need to cite your sources in a Works Cited page in your paper or outline.

## Supporting Your Ideas

As you write your speech, you will need to support the ideas you put forth. There are four types of supporting material.

### Definition

A definition gives a specific explanation of a specific term or idea. Using definitions helps to ensure your audience understands the concepts you are discussing. A definition does not necessary mean you are using a dictionary or encyclopedia. You can define terms in your own words.

### Example

An example is a specific case used to illustrate a term or concept. Examples can be brief (three types of fish are bass, trout, and grouper) or extended. Extended examples provide more detail and could include stories or anecdotes. Examples clarify information and can add interest to a speech.

> **RESEARCH TRIVIA**
>
> Adapted from the *Chapter-by-Chapter Guide to the Art of Public Speaking*.
>
> Find the answers to the following questions. You must use at least one of each: internet, library catalog, and library databases. For each, include your answer and where you found the information
>
> 1. What award did author Toni Morrison win in 1993?
> 2. Whom did the University of North Carolina defeat, and by what score, to win the 1996 NCAA women's soccer championship?
> 3. Who said, "When one is a stranger to oneself then one is estranged too"?
> 4. What is the average annual rainfall of the following cities: Nashville, London, Lima, and Tokyo?
> 5. Movies based on what book have been remade most often?
> 6. Where does the term "hysterical" come from?
> 7. How many states does the Mississippi River touch?
> 8. What are the four Noble Truths of Buddhism?
> 9. What two U.S. Presidents died on July 4th, 1826?
> 10. How much gold stands behind each American dollar?

### Statistics

Statistics are numerical data. Statistics can also clarify information and provide specific data to a speech. When using statistics, it is important to round off the numbers to create ease of understanding for your audience. You also want to avoid overusing statistics, as numbers can fail to make sense when too many are used. You may consider using a visual aid to assist in comprehension of the statistics you use.

### Testimony

A testimony is a direct quote or paraphrase from a specific person. A direct quote should be used only when it is concise and comments on the specific idea you are addressing. This again can add interest. Testimonies can also add credibility, as you have information from a particular source that supports your claims. The person you cite should be an expert on your topic and you should provide his or her name and title when stating the testimony within your speech.

## ANALYZING YOUR AUDIENCE

Audience analysis is the process of evaluating those to whom you will be speaking. Although you will not be able to gain personal knowledge of each person in the audience, you can achieve an overview of the basic demographics. Consider factors such as age, gender, race and socio-

Communication and Research  69

> **AUDIENCE ANALYSIS ACTIVITY**
>
> Below are six speech topics. Decide on the most effective method to relate each to your classmates in a way that will be interesting to them.
>
> Social Security         Laughter
> Illiteracy              Steroids
> Soap operas             Blood donation

economic status. You may also consider commonalities that exist among your audience. For instance, every person to whom you will be speaking in this class is a student. Once you have analyzed these aspects, you can look to shared values or concerns that might exist among your audience.

Audience analysis can assist you in many ways as you prepare your speech. First, it may help as you select and develop your topic. Is your topic one that is of interest to your audience? How can you relate your topic to each person so that they will be interested in what you say? How does it impact them? It can also help as you develop your content. What is the most effective way to approach the topic? Consider the audience's knowledge of the topic. How much background information will you need to include? What aspects of your topic are most likely to appeal to the audience? What language is appropriate? You want to ensure your audience will understand you and will not be confused by slang or jargon. You also do not want to offend your audience with your topic or your language. An audience that is offended is one that is not paying attention. You should always have your audience in mind as you plan your speech.

## VISUAL AIDS

Visual aids can provide added impact and clarity to your speech. They are also helpful in adding interest and can improve your credibility with your audience. For a visual aid to be effective, it should add to the speech and be incorporated into the content. There are several types of visuals you can use. The table below includes the types of visuals and the benefits of each.

| Type of Visual Aid | Benefits |
| --- | --- |
| Pictures and Objects | Clarity, interest |
| Maps and Models | Clarity, interest |
| Charts and Graphs | Highlights main points, clarifies statistics |
| Video | Clarity, interest |
| PowerPoint | Clarity, interest, highlights main points |

Visual aids should be clear and large enough for the audience to see and read. If not, they are not effective. Visuals should also be neat and professional. Consider using the computer as opposed to writing or drawing it out by hand. When typing, avoid decorative font and all capital lettering as they are harder to read. If you use PowerPoint, it should only be used to highlight your main ideas, not include everything you will say. Generally, you should limit the information on any visual aid. Too much information can overwhelm the audience and diminish the effectiveness of the visual.

When you present the visuals, there are also some factors to consider. First, your visual aid should be incorporated and discussed during the speech. Take the time to explain the visual. Next, your visual aid should only be displayed while you are discussing it. Otherwise it can be distracting for the audience. Also, remember, the visual aid is there for the audience, not for you. You should know the information included on the visual and not have to rely on reading it. When used effectively, visual aids can provide many benefits to your speech.

## DELIVERY OF SPEECHES

After you have written your speech, you will need to consider how you will deliver it. There are several factors to consider including which delivery method you will use and your verbal and nonverbal delivery. There are four methods of delivery that can be used.

Manuscript speeches are read word for word. The State of the Union address is an example of a manuscript speech. The President uses a teleprompter and is able to read the speech as he delivers it. Manuscript style delivery allows you to have your entire speech written out but does have drawbacks. It can limit eye contact with your audience and can often result in a monotone voice. Memorized speeches are memorized word for word. This can allow you to maintain eye contact without the need for notes, but is very difficult to accomplish. It can also create a rushed, monotone delivery. Impromptu speeches involve little or no preparation. Impromptu speeches can be creative and allow you to "wing-it" but can be difficult to perform well. Most speeches need to be planned ahead. Extemporaneous speeches are those that are planned and practiced but the exact wording is chosen at delivery. With these speeches, the speaker should know the content and organization of the speech well but may still rely on note cards to assist them as they move through the speech. Extemporaneous speeches are generally more dynamic than the other styles as they aim for a conversational style of delivery.

### *Verbal Delivery*

You will need to consider the verbal aspects of your speech as you prepare. Formal speeches call for formal language. The use of slang and jargon should be avoided. If you use terms your audience may be unfamiliar with, be sure you provide a definition to ensure they will understand. You will also want to avoid words that could be offensive to your audience, such as cursing and racist or sexist language.

Another factor to consider is pronunciation. You will want to make sure you are able to pronounce the words you use correctly. Failing to do so can lower the audience's opinion of your credibility. If you are unsure, look up the correct pronunciation and practice it aloud until you are comfortable.

## *Nonverbal Delivery*

Your nonverbal delivery can have a large impact on your speech. It can make your speech more interesting to hear and keep your audience involved with your topic. If poorly delivered, your speech can become boring or full of distractions. There are several nonverbal areas to consider.

## *Paralanguage and Vocal Variety*

Vocal variety refers to the natural variety we employ when we speak. There are three dimensions of vocal variety. First is volume, the loudness at which you speech. You must speak loud enough that your audience can hear you, but not so loud that you are shouting. Rate is how fast you speak. If too fast, it is easy to lose your audience but speaking too slow can be boring. Pitch is the highness or lowness of speaking. If you lack variety of pitch, you will be monotone. The key is to attempt to maintain your natural speaking style as you deliver your speech.

You also want to make sure you speak clearly and avoid mumbling or trailing off as you speak. Finally, don't be afraid to pause. We pause naturally as we talk. Of course too many will make your speech feel choppy, but a brief pause can communicate to your audience that you are moving from one main idea to another and will help your audience follow along as you move through your speech. You should try to avoid vocalized pauses, such as um, uh, er, you know, like, etc. We often use these as filler when we need to pause to collect our thoughts. Instead, try to simply pause, look at your notes and then continue.

## *Eye Contact*

Eye contact is an essential part of delivering a speech. The benefits are numerous; it adds credibility, helps keep your audience involved, allows you to receive feedback from your audience during your presentation, and requires you keep your head up and your voice directed out to your audience, which makes it easier for your audience to hear you. Keeping your head down, reading or looking at the floor, walls, or ceiling all impede eye contact. Although it may be difficult, try not to rely on your notes and work on maintaining eye contact with your entire audience.

## Body Movements

As you deliver your speech, you will need to be aware of your kinesics. First, when you make a formal presentation, your posture should be formal as well. This means you stand up straight and avoid leaning on the desk or podium as you speak. If you plan to move around as you speak, make sure you move with purpose and don't move too quickly. Otherwise, it may appear as though you are moving aimlessly or pacing. Facial expressions should be appropriate to the material you are covering or it could harm the audience's perception of your sincerity as you talk.

Hand gestures are also included here. Gestures can be used to emphasize your points as you speak. However, using too many gestures can be distracting to your audience. Try to avoid waving your arms and hands, particularly when using note cards as they can emphasize the movements.

## Appearance

Generally, when making a formal speech, your appearance should be neat and professional. Your instructor may enforce guidelines for your attire and you should be aware of requirements and any prohibited items. You should avoid wearing clothing that could be distracting. This can include clothes with writing or pictures, particularly unusual clothing, or attire that is revealing. Your goal is not to get the audience to look at you or your clothes, but to listen to you.

## Avoid Fidgeting

This is easier said than done. Most fidgeting arises from nervousness and often we are not conscious of our actions. Fidgeting comes in many forms: rocking, hitting note cards or hands on the desk, adjusting clothing, pushing hair back, etc. Becoming conscious of these behaviors is the first step in eliminating them. Once you are aware of your fidgeting habits, you may be able to find ways to help you avoid them. For instance, if you mess with your hair, try to pull it back away from your face. Don't take a pencil or pen with you as you speak. If you play with your necklace, don't wear it on the day you present. I actually had one student who had the tendency to step back and forth from one foot to the other. She decided to put rather large stones in each shoe so that she would be less likely to do so.

Another issue to remember is that you should not have anything in your mouth when you make your presentation. Get rid of gum or candy before you speak. Both can make it more difficult to speak clearly. Both can also be unattractive and distracting. If you are concerned about dry mouth, take some water up with you (being mindful of any computers or electrical equipment) and take small sips as needed.

As previously mentioned, much fidgeting is the result of nerves. The best thing you can do to help prevent nervousness is to practice. Knowing your speech well will allow you to feel more comfortable with the material and eliminate many of the concerns that often arise from feeling unprepared. Review the section about speaking apprehension to discover further helpful information.

Lucas, Stephen E. *The Art of Public Speaking, 6th Ed, Instructor's Manual.* St. Louis: McGraw-Hill, 1998.

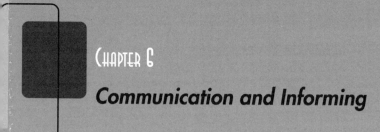

# Chapter 6

## Communication and Informing

### INTRODUCTION

**Informative speaking** as the name implies gives information. In this section we will look at some examples of informative writing and speaking. Note that informative speaking is significantly different than persuasive speaking. Both are content-intensive but informative speaking requires **high interest** and **careful organization** to get the message across. A piece of informative writing (such as a poor technical manual) may have all the information albeit in all the wrong places. A person may have to hunt through it, and even if it is badly organized, they may still find what they need. The same is not true of informative speaking. A poorly organized and dull informative speech may soon lose the listener. Informative speaking is trickier than informative writing. It demands an audience centered approach and attention to detail, specific examples, and interest producing material. No one is under any obligation to listen to most speakers so knowing about audiences can help informative speaking.

### AUDIENCE ANALYSIS

#### Demographics

Audiences are composed around what marketers call demographics, a series of qualities and traits that can be reduced down to simple coded data. For example, **age** is a simple and easy to find **demographic** that can explain many aspects of audience response. A younger audience is theoretically more experimental and less cautious about changing ideas and their personal tastes in clothing and culture. Senior citizens are touted for their good sense and conservative values. **Gender** is used in day time advertisements on television. Although women rival men in the work force, day time advertisers still target women as the stay at home audience. This is an inaccurate perception, but one that relates to the way women used time in the earlier twentieth century.

#### Interests

Themes and audience interest groups play a role in how communication activities are arranged. ESPN has targeted a mostly male sports interested audience. Lifetime courts an affluent older female audience with films, talk shows, and informational programming. Nicktoons targets young people who enjoy animated programming. These niche markets offer communication and programming around themes and ideas that certain groups are likely to enjoy. This **segmenting of the market** is probably an outgrowth of Americans' growing specialization of interest and employment area. We progressively have a less common popular culture and a wider range of **niche cultures**.

## Masters of Informative Speaking

### Newscasters

From **Walter Cronkite** to Peter Jennings to Tom Brokow, newscasters have mastered the style of speaking news in a manner that commands respect and provides information with little bias. Note: the classic newscaster's direct and unbiased approach has been challenged in recent years by opinionated broadcasts by Dan Rather, *Fox News* and *Crossfire*. Though opinion shows draw large ratings, provide thrilling controversy, and excite and polarize audiences, in the end they may be less valuable than straight news programming because they distort information, inflame audiences, sow discord, and provide more heat than light. In the end, they provide less information, distort information so rational choices can not be made objectively by audiences, and eventually throw so much debris in the field of information that good choices often cannot be made. Most senior newscasters are also editors of news material and they learn how to tell stories in compelling and exciting ways. This can be done with drama, great voices, and sparkling arrangements of data. Sadly, this skill is overlooked.

### Scientists

The famous astronomer, **Carl Sagan** comes to mind as a great speaker who used knowledge to stimulate an entire generation of young people to study Physics, Astronomy, and Space. Though continually criticized for his emphasis on "billions and billions of worlds," Sagan's use of statistical, numerical, and physical knowledge contrasted with speakers only supported by opinions. Certainly, Sagan was also opinionated, but for the most part his opinions were supported by facts.

Another more recent example of the power of scientific thought to inspire and entertain is William Peterson's compelling character of **Gill Grissom from CSI**. While the program often has violent subject matter and gruesome dead bodies, the way this material is used helps us decode important information, clues, and information that can lead to ideas about murderers and more generally to a greater understanding of science and forensic medicine. Peterson's character is a kind of a nerd who listens to classical music, constantly studies new skills, learns from careful observation, rarely becomes angry or unfocused, and doggedly pursues the guilty without malice or threats. He represents the best of popular culture's ideas of Sherlock Holmes and Mr. Spock, and he rarely allows the jaded surroundings of Las Vegas to invade his process. Someone who seems to live less and watch more, Peterson's portrayal suggests that careful looking and scanning is action.

## INFORMATIVE SPEAKING

### The Thesis

Here is a suggested format and some guidelines that the informative speaker can use. The Thesis is intensely important to the success of strong informative speaking. For example, a speech simply describing the presidency could be dull and difficult to observe, but a speech chronicling the copious achievements of FDR could be invigorating. Specificity does wonders for interest. Always make it specific. The thesis does many things including defining, limiting, and organizing the discussion. First a thesis guarantees that the talk does not wander from one general idea to another. Students often shoot themselves in the foot by talking about movies in general, instead of discussing one pivotal and important film. Which sounds more exciting? A speech on the film *Titanic* or a speech just about movies in general?

> Boring Movies: *Titanic*
> Interesting Movies: *Memento*

Even if you didn't like the movie, *Titanic* (I didn't for many reasons: acting, plot, dialogue, lack of effects, length, originality, etc.), there is a lot more to say about one specific film than the open book and nebulousness of all films for all time.

### Limiting a Topic

The thesis makes sure the topic is cut down to size. Again, if I tried to talk about all film for all time, I would be speaking for many semesters, not the five minutes that most speech students routinely receive. Limitations are good. They allow the student and professor to come to grips with a smaller object. If for example, a student chose **The Phantom Menace** as a feature film to discuss, they have already narrowed what will be discussed. The topics can now be narrowed to:

> Science fiction/action films,
> Large budget films,
> Recent films, and
> Successful films.

All of these limitations give the student a chance to say something really **significant** about the film. They could talk about the bad acting. They could talk about the lack of adult stars (Liam Nissan and Ewen Mcgregor). They could talk about the goofy childish make-up. They could talk about the slow pace and meandering plot. They could discuss the racist use of stereotypes for all villains in the film. Each and every one of these topics would by itself make a great speech.

Finally the thesis helps the student to **organize thoughts.** Again, if one takes film as a topic, one could break a simple film into units. For example, John Ford's classic western, The Searchers explores events before an Indian raid, the impact of the raid itself and the long aftermath of the attack that reveals a strong theme of racism. A thesis that expresses that: The Searchers is divided into three parts to expose the theme of racism, ends up being far stronger and better organized than a thesis that explains that 'The Searchers is a Western.' Duh, really?

Something many people notice instantly is the slim gap between **persuasion and informative speaking**. The difference is one of emphasis. The informative speaker focuses mainly on the information. The persuasive speaker centers attention on the opinion. The speaker informing about Titanic, Phantom Menace and The Searchers might talk in a manner mainly giving information about the films, but just as I have opinions about all three, it is likely that opinions and support for opinions will still play a role even when the ostensive purpose is to give information.

## TYPES OF SPEECHES

There are at least three distinct types of informative speeches and probably more if we list various hybrid forms. Most informative speeches can be seen as demonstration, exposition, or definition speeches.

### *Demonstration*

**Demonstration speeches** are usually called the bake-a-cake school of speaking. Much of the work is done for the speaker by chronological order. For example in the classic high school bake-a-cake speech the cake must be mixed before baking. This makes things easy. Too often it also makes things boring. A problem with these forms of speeches is that they sound routine, and uneventful or simply bland and uninteresting. For example, unless I was about to bake a cake, I would have little interest in the traditional bake a cake speech. These speeches are often referred to as process or process analysis speeches because they describe a process. Now I might be much more receptive to a process speech if it discussed something threatening or pleasing. Perhaps a speech on how to detonate a nuclear device or how to make one's self irresistible to the opposite sex would gain a wider audience. In any case, while easy to construct, the so-called process/demonstration speech can be difficult for audience interest and sameness.

## Definition

Speeches that define something can also run the risk of sounding routine. Sometimes the perspective taken on these types of topics can save the topic from averageness. For example, Ray Bradbury described his childhood at a speech I attended years ago at Occidental College. Although his talk was the standard 'defining what a writer does and how he works,' Bradbury brilliantly wove examples that held the entire audience in awe. Recently Jacques Derrida speaking at Vanderbilt did a similar thing. He came to speak about perjury, a legal term, something sort of dry and dull in actual testimony, but the venerable philosopher rose to the occasion lifting examples from stories by Andre Malraux and others so that the new definition of perjury was an act of redefining and explored possibilities that lawyers rarely think of in that word.

## Exposition

When most people think of **description**, they think of expository speeches or speeches that describe an object, process, event, or concept. The classic object description from a student is probably their car. Though this might seem quite routine, it has often been revealing and amusing, because what the student invests in their 1967, two-door, three-tone, dented, five-speed, six-cylinder rat trap is obviously colored by a love of their personal transportation beast. Clearly personalizing the object and pointing out distinguishing characteristics that make that object unique gives the audience additional reason to gain interest and listen. Sometimes the power of a unique object can itself demand audience attention. A particularly arresting object is a painting by Picasso entitled *Les demoiselles d' Avignon*. Many suggest it as one of the beginnings of modern art, and it is truly a remarkable and stunning work filled with images of abstraction and primitive form.

Of course **processes** can also be demonstration speeches, but a process can also make a good expository speech, particularly if the process is rich with possibilities for investigation. The process of an election for instance allows the audience to watch with the speaker how an election process starts, produces surprises, and finishes. Looking at a typical election would be duller than dull, but the documentary, *The War Room* takes the Bush/Clinton presidential race and turns it into a vibrant battle ground of strategists and counter strategists. The film makes an election into a literal war zone. At the same time it makes election work seem like fun.

Sometimes **events** are equally bracing and can make great description speeches. My experience at the airplane monument in Kitty Hawk, North Carolina, gave me new respect for the pioneers of flight,

Photo courtesy of Library of Congress

the Wright Brothers. The monument is large and impressive but its strategic location on windy Kill Devil Hill shows onlookers the distance the Brothers had to take their tiny aircraft to prove that flight could work. Just looking at models on the scene and exploring the hill takes one on a journey back through time. You clearly see the two bicycle engineers hard at work perfecting their flying apparatus, and the trials of getting their mechanical bird up and down the hill was of course no mean feat either. Probably the hardest thing to explain is a concept, such as the **Sapir-Whorf hypothesis** discussed by linguists and language scholars. Simply, Sapir–Whorf postulates that language and thinking are related. If you have a word for something you can think about it, and if you don't, well then either you create a word or thinking becomes more difficult. The point of the theory is that thinking and word use are related. Great examples of this exist in literature such as the book, 1984. There the thesis is shown brilliantly through the *Newspeak Dictionary,* a dictionary that every year eliminates words.

## RHETORICAL MODES

Rarely do we discuss the power of rhetorical modes to aid us in supporting good informative speeches, but they can be a key to our success. Let's take a simple and popular topic for informative speaking, and see how we can apply rhetorical modes to this topic to make it more exciting. Many students are interested in the career of evil dictator Adolph Hitler. This notorious character has generated hundreds of books because of the depth of carnage he wrought on the Earth. Time named him one of the men of the century, not because he had done anything positive, but because he plunged the world into a monstrous war. Let's look at the ways we could use rhetorical modes to view Hitler.

> **Comparison.** Hitler could be compared to Franklin Roosevelt or Winston Churchill.
> **Contrast.** Hitler could be contrasted with another dictator like Stalin or Mussolini.
> **Analysis.** One could do a psychoanalytic portrayal of Hitler's mental state explaining the dementia that made him so alluring to German people, but so deadly to world politics.

**Exemplification.** One could list the atrocities such as the holocaust and the violence against other European peoples that were perpetrated in Hitler's regime.
**Process.** One could chronologically show Hitler's quick rise to power in the dangerous times of the world wide depression. The process he went through to eliminate his foes and to build strategic alliances that placed him in the seat of government only eight years after being arrested as a rebel.

Photo courtesy of Library of Congress

**Narration.** One could narrate a fake diary of a madman, a story of Hitler's life as told by the character that lived it.
**Description.** It is always telling to know about someone's physical look. Many people have commented on Hitler's physical size and how he wore his clothing. These things give us an insight into the whole person.
**Cause and Effect.** What caused Hitler's success despite the fact that he was clearly insane? How did the actions of Hitler create the modern map of the European world. What might have been different if he hadn't have lived?
**Argument and Persuasion.** While argument is usually identified with persuasive speaking, one could argue about the value of one particular battle in Hitler's campaign to take over Europe and draw conclusions about Hitler from that example.
**Chronological.** Often used to chart a process, chronological order also tells us about the trajectory of someone's career. Hitler's meteoric rise to power was paralleled by extreme excesses that led to horrible crimes and a massive loss of life.

## PATTERNS

When constructing an informative address, order can help to organize the impact of the address. **Spatial order** means where things are situated in geographical locales. Kentucky is west of Virginia. New York is south of Vermont. Simple but effective, spatial order gives us real world references.

**Temporal order** or time order is something that our current educational system has neglected. Few people know when things happened or what came before what. The problem is that we can't place anything, if we don't know when other things occurred. A group of students were once asked when the Civil War took place. Most could not tell, but few even guessed the correct century.

**Thematic order** is an arrangement pattern that helps place things in a certain genre or theme. For example, if we wanted to place horror movies in theme order we might start with Dracula and vampire movies, move to zombie movies and finally Frankenstein styles of films. Each is a separate theme with an individual history and set of distinctive films. Zombie films were about in the silent era although most people think of zombie films starting with George Romero's *Night of the Living Dead*. This method of classification adds structure and interest simultaneously.

A good thematic order speech might be based on classifications of television shows. Imagine all the teen-oriented shows in recent years: *Buffy, Angel, Gillmore Girls, Lizzie McGuire, Dawson's Creek*. A thesis around the idea that these shows constitute a force and mean something could make an interesting speech. For example, Gillmore Girls is the lighter side of the teen years where Buffy focuses on teenage nightmares coded as vampires, ghosts, and creatures.

Could you clarify that? Suggestions for giving information when speaking.

First, **do not assume the audience knows anything.** With the decline in newspapers, sporadic tv viewing, and radio and television babble, it is possible that audiences know less than they previously did about most things. Take time to explain things completely and thoroughly. Make things clear. **Avoid techno-babble**. Do not use or refer to technical terms that common people will not know unless you carefully explain their meaning. You might know what a 4RTY56 Sproket composer is but most people would not know.

Avoid Abstraction: be specific
Relate the subject to the audience
Personalize

## *Functions of Informative Speaking*

These functions are important when:

1. Sharing information and ideas. You wish to introduce new ideas and knowledge of a subject.
2. Shaping audience perceptions. You want to prepare listeners for future persuasive messages by revealing a situation they have not been aware of.
3. Setting the agenda. You wish to make listeners realize a topic is important and merits their serious consideration.
4. Clarifying options for action.

## Preparing for a Briefing

1. Always be prepared to report in a meeting.
2. Keep your remarks short and to the point.
3. Start with a preview and end with a summary.
4. Have no more than three main points.
5. Use facts and statistics, expert testimony, brief examples, and comparison and contrast for emphasis.
6. Avoid technical jargon.
7. Present your report with assurance.
8. Be prepared to answer tough questions.

# SPEAKING AND STORYTELLING

## Storyteller

Prior to the advent of mass media, the people listened to storytellers and entertained themselves by reading and speaking aloud in small groups. When we go back to Greek culture, we have the hymn praise singer or dithyrambist. The dithyramb was the song of praise to the gods, and the singer was both an entertainer and worshipper. He led a group of chorus members who also sang to the gods.

African tribes had storytellers, healers, witch doctors who sat in circles and encouraged the people through ceremonies of healing and songs of praise. Here the emphasis was on sharing ideas and the leader listened as well as spoke to the people. Together chants were called out in rhythmic fashion and the drum was used as a ritual tool to bind all the tribe in one communal rhythm. This tribal drumming was complex and the movements of the tribal dance were thought to bring the audience chorus or tribe members into rhythmic harmony with the world, the gods and the fellow tribe members. The audience was receptive to the sacred stories in both Greek and African cultures.

In North America, the storytellers or wise men **shamans** also sat in circles and listened to tribal matters as a healing, often governmental body of elders. In fact the circular configuration to sitting and listening is almost a universal. Asian and Chinese performers would establish a performance space by simply drawing a circle to outline the area of the performance space. Similarly the Greeks built theatres in the semi-circular form. Shakespeare's globe was circular. The roman Forum and coliseum were built on circular models. Even modern German playwright Bertolt Brecht returned to the ancient Chinese performance circle in his play, *The Caucasian Chalk Circle* suggesting the transposition of the ancient Chinese method of communication back to the Occidental Western culture.

Today, **storytellers** arrive in all shapes and forms from TV talk show hosts to story hours for children at local libraries. But the art of listening to others speaking had been endangered by a lack of time and focus in our society. Recently the growth of cassette and CD talking books where people actually read books aloud has begun to slightly reverse the trend. For modern commuters who have little time for luxurious reading schedules, the use of talking books is a fine way to utilize drive time and restore the lost art of listening. Too bad we can't interact with the storyteller in a talking book, but someday we might. Consider the enormous long term success of Garrison Keillor's *Prairie Home Companion*. Based on the model of the *Grand Ole' Oprey* shows of the 20s and 30s, Keillor wrestles with ways to make the radio of the past vibrant for today's listeners. He uses humor, hymns, church culture, small town American life and parody (Guy Noir, the world's worst radio detective) to make points about American life. He tells Republican and Democrat jokes.

## THE PHILOSOPHY OF INFORMING

In a famous parody of a famous ad group, there is a picture of a group of sheep all sporting red, white, and blue accessories. Then in the corner there is a Tommy Hilfiger symbol. The sense of the parody is that anyone caught wearing this brand is a sheep and not a thinking person. This parody of a Tommy Hilfiger ad makes fun of brand identity and fashionable consumerism. Sometimes informative speaking and communicating provides information that also states opinion. That's ok, so long as the emphasis is on communication and not simply arguing. Realize that in today's society, many times persuasion substitutes for knowledge. It is so easy for a talk show to have a variety of lively opinions and lots of argument but much harder to produce a show filled with well reasoned knowledge. Knowledge and its presentation requires rigorous research. That's why being a scientist is difficult. By contrast making good arguments or even bad arguments can be at least entertaining and easier with little productively accomplished.

Our society is filled with the idea of **combative dialogue**. While Oprah may have heralded the age of feeling talk, Springer, Oprah, and *Entertainment Tonight* have raised violent outbursts, personal attacks, and gossip to new levels. Women cheer on other women and feel free to denigrate men on some Oprah episodes. Springer encourages stage combat like a wrestling program. Entertainment Tonight has learned to tactfully trash the high and mighty of Hollywood. The problem is that few of these shows offer much in the way of useful valuable information. They offer diversion and emotion. In journalism, the new movement is away from conflict and "gotcha" reports in which someone is made to look bad toward what is termed civic journalism or community reporting. Although the recent inquiry over what President Bush knew prior to 911 is a throwback to that style of reporting, it is largely waning in popularity. Consumers, particularly women have abandoned the press for its **confrontational methodology.** To lure them back, the press is offering pages for working mothers, healthful diet recipes, and job tips for women returning to work. The idea is to provide 'news you can use' and to avoid any subjects that simply push people's buttons. Good? It is important to provide a press that presents content rather than simply accusations. Facts, data, explanations, statistics, materials, sources, websites all allow consumers of information to shop for ideas that empower themselves. This is a new goal for informative writing and speaking, to create what America has lost, namely an informed and knowledgeable citizenry. It is also useful in that it changes our perspective on the news from news being about **STARS** important remote people (Presidents, Middle Eastern people, and New Yorkers) to news being the **events** that happen to everyone around the world, the press of common but newsworthy occurrence: high academic achievement, community ceremonies and religious gatherings, local business and cultural events. This type of reporting used to be termed feature writing because it featured common people, now it's called "community journalism." The downside of common, small town news is pandering to a select audience, the grin-and-grab pictures of teens as homecoming royalty at local high schools, bankers breaking ground, and civic groups saluting their own members occupies small dailies throughout the nation.

## *Informative Examples*

Here is an example of an informative essay that would provide material that would make a good informative presentation.

Example Informative Speech Essay
Name: Student
Time:
Topic: Einstein
Title: *Einstein, Man and Genius*

> *The ideals that have lighted my way, and time after time have given me new courage to face life cheerfully have been Kindness, Beauty, and Truth. . . . the trite subjects of human efforts—possessions, outward success, luxury—have always seemed to me contemptible.*
>
> —Albert Einstein

Photo courtesy of Library of Congress

## Introduction and Thesis

In the wake of continual acts of violence and horror that disrupt the placidity of our daily lives, it is important to contemplate the ideas and people who make life worth celebrating. In my particular class we study communication and it's rich and illustrious history. Some people have simple messages that are remembered for their formal elegance and their clear expression. Yet others have complex minds that are unique and often to many others unfathomable. To the mere common minds these people are geniuses or crazies. One such communicator was Albert Einstein. By all accounts, Einstein is still considered one of the greatest minds if not the greatest mind of the 20th century, but remarkably one of the most difficult to penetrate.

## Support and Examples

Remarkably, Einstein spent a large portion of his life under the intense scrutiny of the public. After his special theory of relativity was published in 1905, he became an international celebrity, and he spent the better part of his remaining fifty years coping with the burdens of popularity. (Fredricks 19) In his newfound status as a public figure, he tried to wield his fame with modesty and reason. When he was old and near death he was invited to celebrate the 50th anniversary of his discovery of relativity and he declined citing health reasons but also explaining that "everything that has anything to do with the cult of personality has always been painful to me." ("Einstein," Biography)

Einstein's contribution to communication is perhaps least remembered but is considerable because of all the thinkers of the 20th century, his subject was perhaps the most esoteric to describe to lay persons. While ideas about relativity and nuclear physics could be seen and felt in practice, few could grasp the insights and theories that led Einstein to his views about how the universe operated.

## Example on Religion

Such a substantial understanding of science causes many to think that Einstein lacked faith in some higher power, but Einstein though not a deeply religious or practicing Jew was nevertheless profoundly excited by religious understanding, placing moral teachers on a plane above mere scientists and technicians. (Einstein "Why Socialism" 13) Einstein didn't lack faith in people either. Despite the horrors of war, Einstein saw man's quest for knowledge as natural and right. "The most incomprehensible thing about the world is that it is comprehensible," he said reassuringly. (Einstein Online)

He was unafraid to speak out to defend those he loved. Though not involved in Zionism for his own sake, he saw the need for a Jewish state to defend Jews from extinction in the world, and he supported Israel's creation. But he himself never chose to live there. ("Einstein" in *Britannica Online*)

**Example on Physics**
What is remarkable about Einstein is the clarity of his theoretical vision. His writings on Physics, though complex to most laymen contained simple profundities like this description mass at rest. "Mass: When we measure the mass of an object by weighing it, we are measuring as its mass at rest the moving mass together with the resting mass of the particles that make it up. There is no such thing as mass totally at rest. Moving mass is resting mass, if it is confined to an infinitesimal volume. Mass at rest is a relative concept." (Einstein Online) How many Harvard English PhD's could have phrased the matter so eloquently?

**Example on Career**
He was offered a position in the early 1930s to come to America and study at the Institute for Advanced Studies at Princeton. When the Nazis assumed power Einstein had no bridges to his homeland and America became his adopted home. But unlike other refugees, Einstein did not look back longingly at his previous life. He set immediately to work and continued his quest for a unified field theory, a means to understand all matter. (Mortimer 36) He had the remarkable ability to be at work on a problem wherever he happened to find himself. His position at Princeton entailed no teaching or research duties (Einstein found published research odious because it led to publishing just for its own sake, not because one had anything really important to say.).

**Example on Humor and Conclusion**
As with all truly great men, Einstein was modest and aware of his limitations, but his profoundly human sense of humor often served him well. A young well wisher wrote asking for his autograph and claimed she would have written sooner but she thought he was dead. Einstein wrote back. "I have to apologize to you that I am still among the living. There will be a remedy for this, however." (Fredricks 418)

## WORKS CITED

Einstein, Albert. "WHY SOCIALISM?" Monthly Review. NY:NY, May, 1949 11-14.

"Einstein." Britannica Online. Vers. 97.1.1. Mar. 1997. Encyclopedia Britannica. 29 Mar. 1997 <http://www.eb.com:180>.

Fredricks, Ben. *The Burden of Genius, Einstein in the 20th Century Mind.* Cambridge, MA: Harvard University Press, 1989.

Friedman, S. Morgan. "Albert Einstein Online." Apr. 1997. Indiana U. 26 Apr. 1997 <http://www.Indiana.edu/~letrs/vwwp/>.

Mortimer, Cathy. "If Einstein Were Alive Today." **U. S. News and World Reports.** June, 1989, 35-36.

"Albert Einstein." Biography. **A&E Cable Network**. 1/96. Broadcast April 17, 1998.

NOTE: How works are cited in MLA style
(1002 words.) This essay has been reduced to fit on two pages. Student essays should be double-spaced and written in 12 point type (no larger). The Works Cited section must contain 5 credible sources (2 internet/2 paper/1 alternative media). The Works Cited must follow the MLA Stylebook. The format for online publications reflected here comes from the MLA online which gives the updated format for citing online sources. Check it out at http://www.mla.org/ for more info on the form.

## KEY TERMS

informative speaking
speeches about objects
speeches about processes
speeches about events
speeches about concepts
informative briefings
technical reports
storytellers
shamans
Garrison Keillor

*Prairie Home Companion*
lecture
question-and-answer session
speaker's sign posts
demographics
age, gender, interests
mnemonic devices
thematic, spatial, temporal order
rhetorical modes

# CHAPTER 7
## Communication and Persuading

### CRITICAL THINKING

#### Visual Argument and Mood Altering Drugs

You've all seen an ad like this. A woman is a cartoon figure and she is feeling uncomfortable, fearful, and nervous. The voiceover explains, "do you feel uncomfortable in social situations? Do you suffer from fear in social situations, timidity and worry that you or your ideas won't be accepted? Do you think people don't like you or find you unattractive? Maybe you suffer from social anxiety disorder and you need _____." After the drug is shown the cartoon image of the woman changes to bright colors. She is dancing. The scene become verdant and forested and all things are better. This is an example of **visual argument. Very little real information** or genuine logic has been used to convince the audience of anything. The **images tell the story** and seek to **bypass logical thought** with either **frightening images or supportive ones.** The term social anxiety disorder is a clever series of words to suggest that feeling bad itself is a type of disease that can be treated with drugs. In reality there is no such disease. It is made up to sound scientific and to present a need that you (the audience) needs to do something about "your condition." In reality feeling bad on occasion is typical and not strange or wrong or especially a disease. The use of positive images at the commercial's end also suggests that once someone takes the drug, the reasons for life's problems will disappear. This is completely untrue. Unless one solves the roots of the feelings, the feelings will persist. We are just beginning to understand the negative effects of mood altering drugs. They cannot permanently fix bad feelings. They can have hidden and deadly side effects. They can suddenly prompt feelings of suicide. Yet since these drugs were authorized as legal, people have widely accepted them because they have seen them advertised on television, and for the most part, **people think that what they see on television is harmless and can't hurt them.**

Today people visit their doctor and demand these drugs. These commercials do what commercials have done effectively for over a hundred years: **they promote a need for something that previously there was no need** or even awareness of prior to the advertisement. More worrisome, the subtle use of visual images makes it hard for audiences to even know they are being marketed to or manipulated by images. The demand is so high that over 60 million prescriptions for mood elevating drugs has been written. In a population of 290 million people, that means that **over one in five people could be relying on a mood altering drug to make their life decisions.**

Thus visual argument is a highly effective and controversial way to sell. The qualities are:

1. **No or little dialogue**
2. **Focus on visual images** over rational arguments
3. **Pictures paint feelings** that the audience either gravitates to or wishes to avoid
4. **The outcomes are exaggerated** in a non-realistic way.
5. **Little effort is given to facts** or realities that could make a person process the information in a rational way.
6. Things that are distortions or **manipulations are presented as realities.**

Here advertisers without actually lying present such a pleasant but ultimately inaccurate view of the world, that people become willing to accept these distortions as realities despite the dangers. Further, there is pressure for profit amongst doctors and pharmaceutical manufacturers to push and market more of these drugs to increase marketshare. Oddly there was a famous book about depression as a mental illness entitled ***Prozac Nation (1999)*** by Elizabeth Wurtzel. It was filmed in 2001 starring famous actresses Christina Ricci and Jessica Lange and licensed by Miramax films *(Shakespeare in Love, Pulp Fiction)*. Weirdly the film was unreleased for four years and finally debuted (or was buried . . ) on the Starz Network in 2005. Visual argument is very powerful and wields lots of economic and social force. It is something modern consumer societies must be vigilant against because **it is easier to be overwhelmed and seduced by pretty pictures than by talk.** Think of those Pepsi or Coke commercials where beautiful young, swim-suited people stand, perfectly fit, smiling, drinking Coke, playing volleyball, and sharing good times with friends. Reality or visual argument?

## *Ethos, Logos, Pathos*

An ethical appeal uses the ethics of the audience to attempt to convince them. For example, the speaker might identify with a popular preacher or use his name to encourage audience members to agree with his arguments. In the 2004 election, Karl Rove, Republican strategist used the ideas of abortion and gay marriage to galvanize fundamentalist voters to vote for President Bush. Instead of the president having to convince voters (something he had difficulty doing in the three logical debates against strong logical debater and challenger, Senator and Vietnam War Hero John Kerry), Rove rallied conservative preachers to discuss those gay and abortion issues with their contributions. The hope was that audiences would so identify with the ethos of their beloved pastors that that love and obedience would become active votes for Bush on those issues. On election day, votes for Bush favored him on those issues. In this instance, ethical appeals to the audience may have been more successful than logic.

Ethical appeals don't always work. After the Watergate scandal President Nixon went before the American people and proclaimed, "I am not a crook." The president suffered from an ethical problem with the public and Nixon was thought to be connected to the Watergate break-ins and was forced to resign his presidency.

Logos is the appeal to logic. This is usually the most successful and viable way to convince an audience. Scientists discussing evolution or global warming submit logical proof and evidence that their ideas are correct. If audiences concur then they are usually respected as having found the correct answer. Sometimes the logic of using scientists can be perverted. For example, there was a television commercial that began, "Hi, I'm not a doctor, but I play one on television." In essence, this actor told the audience not to believe his medical advice, but often times, people who portray physicians are treated like the real thing. The actors on **ER** have often commented on fans and audience members asking them for medical advice. They claim they are just actors only spouting lines, but people think because they play doctors that they are as wise as doctors.

Good scientific logical proof would be when a JPL team determines the right trajectory for a missile launch to another planet. If the missile hits its target it is fairly strong proof that the acts of the scientists were correct.

Finally, pathos is an appeal to emotions. When we see the starving children in commercials for "Feed the Children" and other organizations, the images of suffering helpless children is supposed to make us feel sadness and guilt so that we send money to save these children. A strong emotional appeal is used in Mel Gibson's The Passion. Many people, (myself included) feel the two-and-one-half hour epic is so filled with bloodshed and acts of cruelty that it cannot be deemed pro-Christian, and by its violence and loveless character is a distortion of basic Christian teachings. Defenders of the film argue that the violence is there to illustrate Christ's love and suffering for mankind and the violence must be intense to show the depth of his sacrifice. A logical argument would say that: if **more** violence equals more love for mankind, than perhaps Natural Born Killers, Scarface, and Pulp Fiction are even more holy than The Passion? Whatever the ultimate value of Gibson's bloody epic, The Passion uses emotions to make all people discuss it and its message.

## Ethical Persuasion

**Ethical persuasion seeks to convince us of things for our own good.** Unethical persuasion uses techniques that an be unscrupulous in getting us to adopt a product or a belief. An example of ethical persuasion might be a religious person asking you to give up a self-destructive behavior such as smoking or drug addiction. The persuader has very little to gain by your change in behavior but you and the society stand to gain in a major way. This is good persuasion and seen all to infrequently. When the president urges Americans to conserve fuel, he is trying to preserve precious national resources and he seeks to reduce costs, this can be seen as ethical and to the benefit of all.

Persuasion attempts to change our **attitudes, actions or behavior.** A persuader has to have a clear objective in mind. What do you want the audience to do? Change their voting, buy this product or quit smoking? Without a clear purpose it is hard to convince an audience of anything.

Good persuasion like good writing must begin with a clear objective or thesis. This should be stated explicitly at least for you the persuader. If the persuader feels there may be resistance to an idea's adoption, a persuader may take the path of indirectly persuading. So long as this technique is employed without lying or deceit it can be an effective manner of obtaining an audience's acceptance of idea that they might not otherwise accept. An example of this technique is used in commercials where warm, fuzzy images of mothers and children are shown prior to the actual commercial message. If it happens to be a commercial for a hospital selling medical services it might be deceptive, but if it is prepared by a public service organization like planned parenthood, there is little profit motive involved.

Good persuasion uses reasoning. Two common types of reasoning are deduction and induction.

## Deduction

Deduction is popular because it follows a certain tight pattern. The formal tool of deduction is the syllogism which is based on the three parts:

1. major premise = all men are mortal
2. minor premise = Socrates is a man
3. conclusion = Socrates is mortal

In a syllogism you will notice that the major promise is a major generalization about things we believe to be true. The minor premise is a subset of the major premise. In this case, if we know something about all men, then we are more likely to be able to draw some conclusion about Socrates who happens to be a particular man.

Another example might be the Joe Dante film *Gremlins*. If you remember there are some syllogistic logics stated in that film concerning *Gremlins*. These syllogisms were broken with disastrous consequences. You'll recall the hero is told three things:

1. Don't expose them to bright light.
2. Don't feed them after midnight.
3. Don't get them wet.

# Communication and Persuading

Of course we can follow the logic of the film by seeing what happens. Let's make a syllogism out of the film.

1. Major Premise = If you get the Gremlins wet, there will be consequences
2. Minor Premise = Gizmo (a particular Gremlin) gets wet
3. Conclusion = Gizmo will suffer consequences

To get good deductive logic we have to make certain assumptions, that is things believed to be true. We can test assumptions for validity, validity means the conclusion of an argument cannot be false if the premises are true. We are dependent on the truth of premises and our assumptions to make good syllogistic statements. One simplified form of a syllogism can be an enthymeme, a statement that omits part of the argument.

Good logic is undone by logical fallacies that interfere with clear thinking and good communication. Some common fallacies are:

ambiguity: a word with two or more distinct meanings
vagueness: too broad, no concrete meaning
equivocation: two meanings of a word mixed
obscuration: using big words to obscure the meaning of a word

Good deduction depends on good language, truth, and validity. This combination of factors can create reliable if not foolproof deductions. At best we can look for dependable deductions, but they are never air tight because assumptions, generalizations, and language might be wrong.

## *Induction*

Induction is the opposite of deduction. As deduction works from generalizations and moves to specific examples, induction works by moving from specific examples or a sampling to a generalization. For example to prove deductively that people are mortal we have to know generally that people die and then apply that information to the death of one individual, namely Socrates. Inductively we can get to the same place by seeing examples of people who have died, and conclude that in general people appear to be mortal with limited life expectancies. A little lighter proof would be to survey the number of 16-year-olds that watch *Dawson's Creek*. If we spoke to 100 people in that age group at random and found that over 80 percent watched the show regularly we could safely say that the show appears to be popular with that age group. It's a generalization based on induction but its quite limited.

There are three tests to using specific examples as part of your sampling. First, is the sample known? If we know the source of a sample we can better evaluate its reliability. Is the sample sufficient? Are there enough people/events sampled to be significant? Finally, is the sample representative? Are there many examples like the ones we're seeing or is this an isolated case? Let's say we wish to examine teen drivers. We see lots of teens driving from the high school in our community (a known sample). We know that this is the only high school in the area, so the sampling is sufficient because it represents an overwhelming portion of the teens in our area who drive. Finally, if we see a certain driving behavior exhibited by these teens as they leave school we get a representative group that is likely to be reliable. So this sampling would be good for basing generalizations about teen driving, whether the sampling was good or bad.

## *The Toulmin Model*

The Toulmin Model is another less formal means for testing the reliability of statements/conclusions. The Toulmin Model uses these logical tests in this order:

**grounds**                **to claim to**                **warrant**

Each aspect of the Model helps in the proof. The grounds are the pieces of information collected. The claim is the conclusion drawn from information uncovered. A warrant is the connecting principle linking information to the conclusion.

An example might be the proposition that television is harmful to young people and should be controlled. The claim or inference would be that evidence exists to suggest people repeat antisocial behavior or behavior they see on television. Evidence or the grounds would be that there are lots of crimes committed by young people that have been watching television regularly. The warrant or sub-evidence that connects the grounds to the claim is that many young offenders point to television as the inspirer of their crimes. The value of this model is that people don't speak syllogistically so this system can give a reasoning for coming to conclusions. We must still evaluate warrants for:

1. **support or backing**
2. **rebuttal information**
3. **claim qualifiers that can make a warrant more reasonable**

## DECISION MAKING

Evaluating information is difficult but to make careful decisions one has to examine the premises, consistency, sufficiency, and coherence of the evidence. A sharp decision maker evaluates sources for their validity. Supporting data has to be evaluated for its recentness.

## Critical vs Creative Thinking

Creative thinking involves the imagination, intuition, and brainstorming techniques. While imagination and intuition are difficult to categorize and to cultivate, brainstorming is a skill that can be cultivated.

## Brainstorming

- combines critical/creative
- uninhibited idea generation
- critical examination of ideas

In the life of Einstein creative visualization played a large role in his breakthrough thinking. Einstein could visualize how planets, systems, and constellations might move, or how time might bend back upon itself. His theory of relativity required the ability to reexamine the evidence of a thousand years of astrophysics in a new way and to reinvent physics for the 20th century.

In our decision making plans, we need to identify essential criteria to make informed decisions. Think of what we need to know to make an informed decision. Consider these questions.

> What are the issues that are of the greatest concern to apply critical thinking skills?
> What are these things that are major concerns and why?
> What words and phrases are ambiguous?
> What are the value conflicts and assumptions?
> What are the descriptive assumptions?
> Are there any fallacies in the reasoning?
> How good is the evidence?
> Are there rival causes?
> Are the statistics deceptive?
> What significant information is omitted?
> What reasonable conclusions are possible?

## Propaganda Techniques

Often we are presented with shoddy reasoning and deceptive practices that prevent us from seeing issues clearly. Some things to beware of in reasoning.

1. **Attacks Ad Hominem.** Literally, attacking the man or woman personally, not attacking the argument or the issues themselves. In politics, often campaigns are launched against individuals not against their stands and ideals. This is bad thinking and cuts off reasonable debate. It substitutes prejudices and irrational beliefs for real understanding.

2. **Post Hoc Ergo Propter Hoc.** Literally, after this then that. This fallacy suggests that because something preceded something else in time, it must have caused it. If I eat a hamburger in Phoenix and there is an earthquake in LA, it is highly unlikely that the two events are connected even though one may have come before the other. Sometimes cause and effect relationships are used to manipulate people. Hitler blamed Germany's problems on the Jewish population of that country. There was no evidence that Germany's problems were in any way connected with the people of the Jewish faith. In fact Jews had been connected with Germany through its times of greatest prosperity and Jewish citizens along with all Germans suffered equally after WWI. Many factors affected Germany after the war, war reparation, inflation, weak government, etc. but Hitler's reasoning that something coming before something else just because one existed before the other was flawed and irrational thinking.

3. **False Cause.** Something is assumed to have caused something else, even though the two issues were not related. For example, Oliver Stone comments in *JFK* that nothing was right in America after JFK died. This assumes that the death of one man could adversely affect the fortunes of a whole country. This is unlikely to be true, regardless of who the man or the country are.

4. **Too Many Questions; Masquerading as One.** "Are you the anarchist responsible for blowing up multiple bridges?" This question presupposes that the subject is an anarchist and that that person is responsible for multiple acts. The subject cannot answer a simple yes or no.

5. **Red Herring.** Introducing an issue that is not relevant to the discussion or debate. A murder is investigated and someone claims to have seen a person that doesn't exist at the scene of the crime. The claimant is throwing a red herring or false evidence at the case.

6. **Oversimplification.** Assuming that a simple cause creates a complex result. D-Day ended WWII. This is an oversimplification. The invasion of Normandy on D-Day certainly hastened the war's end but the Battle of the Bulge, Hiroshima, the Italian campaign, the middle Eastern War and events in Russia all played a part in the war's conclusion.

7. **False Claim.** Assuming something that is not true to be true. Commercials make claims that often cannot be substantiated. Diet drinks will make you lose weight and feel great. Are these claims true? Maybe not.

8. **Poisoning the Well.** Judging an argument not by the quality of its reasoning but by its origins. If someone argued for the nationalization of some industry on the grounds that it would bet-

Communication and Persuading 97

ter serve the public interest, then that might be a valid argument. But if someone countered that argument by saying nationalization was also a Nazi policy this would be poisoning the well or throwing doubt on the concept because of it's origins.

9. **Appeal to Authority.** Jefferson owned slaves so slave owning must be alright, no? To appeal to an authority figure to show the rightness of an otherwise flawed argument is a fallacy.

10. **The Slippery Slope.** If we legalize marijuana then soon everyone will become a drug addict. This type of fallacy assumes that one thing leads to another conclusion. This is not true. If we followed that logic with legalizing drinking then supposedly everyone would be an alcoholic.

11. **Appeal to Ignorance.** Arguments for the death penalty say it is a deterrent from murder, but we don't know how many people have actually been deterred by threat of death. Can one argue for something on the basis of what one doesn't know? No!

12. **Begging the Question.** Assuming a premise to be true. I drive the speed limit because I believe in the law. Not necessarily so. I might be driving the speed limit because I don't have the money to pay for a ticket. If we assume a premise to be true that we are trying to prove then this is begging the question. A simpler example of a conclusion masquerading as a premise is the statement, "I'm right because I say I'm right." The premise to prove the conclusion is the same as the conclusion. Can you assume something is true and use it to prove that it is true?

13. **Suppressed Alternatives.** When an audience is confronted with a false set of two alternatives when many more may exist. "Either we ban drugs or outlaw them." What about education? Reduced penalties for some drugs, harsher for others? There are many other alternatives.

14. **Equivocation** (equal voice). Two people using the same word but using two different meanings of it.

15. **False Analogy.** Something is like something else when it is not.

Critical thinking is defined as an: Awareness of a set of interrelated questions that discover the truth and validity of a given proposition. One must have the ability to ask and answer these questions at appropriate times.

One must have a desire to use critical questions effectively.

Some basic critical thinking questions that can be applied to good rhetoric and argument:

1. Is the proposition reasonable or likely? Can the logic of the argument be mapped, drawn or diagrammed?
2. Are there at least two clear sides to this issue?

3. What are the facts in this case?
4. Is the reasoning behind this speaker's stand clear and rational?
5. What flaws if any exist in reasoning?
6. How strong is the evidence/proof?
7. What is factually wrong in this case?
8. What support is offered to substantiate claim?
9. What conclusions could be drawn on topic?

Passive learning is effective for sponge learning, that is absorbing a quantity of data, but there are disadvantages such as no ability to screen out unwanted data. Some types of learning require an active 'panning for gold' approach. This type of learning involves making critical/judgmental decisions including asking questions to determine the validity of statements.

Good learners have a variety of skills they use to answer questions. One myth that many learners encounter is that there is only one right answer. It also helps to be able to ask questions first and to deal with emotions later. This keeps the thinking geared towards logical analysis which helps with most practical issues. Emotions can cloud an otherwise simple decision.

Sometimes critical thinking skills should be reserved for only important matters. To apply critical thinking skills to every decision would be pointless. Who cares about every issue? Apply critical thinking skills judiciously! There are weak and strong critical thinking skills that are apparent all the time. When people simply attempt to defend the status quo that is weak critical thinking. When they use such skills to prove the truth, then that is good critical thinking.

## *Criteria for Judging a Sound Argumentative Address*

1. Logic: Does the speaker sound like he or she is making a rational, logical argument?
2. Does the reasoning contain any fallacies?
3. Are there false claims or unsubstantiated claims?
4. Does the speaker use sources and references to prove a point? How trustworthy are these references?
5. Is the address a paid announcement? That is, is it an advertisement?
6. What is the speaker's motive in the address?
7. What is the order of the speech? Is there a series of main points that can be charted or arranged in an order, or does the speech seem chaotic and random?
8. Does the speaker use a prepared manuscript or notes?

## ORWELL AND PERSUASION

Perhaps the most famous writer about persuasion and bad thinking in the twentieth century was George Orwell. In his famous essay, "Politics and the English Language," he made the tangible connection that bad word use and bad speaking and writing resulted in bad politics. The converse was also true. Poor political use of language would result in a decline in language. Orwell writes of language that "It becomes ugly and inaccurate because our thoughts are foolish, but the slovenliness of our language makes it easier for us to have foolish thoughts." The sloppiness of language use creates bad thinking and then bad thinking makes it easier to use language is a less artful way. This is a downward spiral, but Orwell thinks its reversible if we become aware of it. Orwell has two gripes that he argues makes writing less meaningful. "The first is staleness of imagery; the other is lack of precision." Writing that uses phrases without thinking, and writing that doesn't become very accurate.

He refers to these linguistic illnesses as four problems, and they are worth repeating.

1. **Dying Metaphors.** These are words that used to refer to something but no longer have meaning for most people. Dead as a door knob. This used to mean something but most people have forgotten what that thought referred to in visual terms.

2. **Operators or Verbal False Limbs.** These are words that appear to say something but really say nothing at all. "It appears to all the parties concerned that the seriousness of the matter requires a solution." It would be simpler to cut out the middle and just say: "It appears the matter requires a solution." The other words are operators and don't say much.

3. **Meaningless Words.** "We want to give the people freedom from their tyrannical enemies." Words like enemy and freedom are meaningless. Who is the enemy? Does the enemy change over time? Who are our friends? Do they change over time?

4. **Pretentious Diction.** A term that comes to mind is the phrase **activist judges.** This term is used by conservative critics against judges who side with progressive causes. It is pretentious because it suggests that only progressives are activists and conservatives are never activist. The truth is that both conservatives and progressives are constantly acting as activists to promote one agenda or another. Lots of terms are pretentious now. **"Hero"** Anyone involved in a big dangerous event is a hero.

All victims in 911, all soldiers in all wars, and all firemen and police are now heroes. This use of the word diminishes the meaning of the word? Are the 19 planners of the 911 attacks heroes? They died in a war fighting a power they felt strongly about? You see the other side of terms like hero is that they are extremely **subjective.** A terrorist to us, could be a hero to someone in another country opposed to us. Or our soldiers who may have killed over 100,000 Iraqis (figures by Amnesty International) might not be considered heroes in Iraq but might be considered terrorists or oppressors by those people.

Orwell argued that language should be brief, vibrant and clear. He said (speaking after WWII) that, "in our time, political speech and writing are largely the defense of the indefensible."

# Chapter 8
## Communication Interpersonally

As a speech communication instructor, I am often asked why communication courses are required. I hear comments such as "I already know how to talk" or "I'm not going to have give speeches in my job." However, communication is an essential part of our lives. From the time we are born until we pass away, we are communicating. We need communication to receive nourishment, form relationships, accomplish goals and to learn what we need to know in order to survive. Communication is such a vital part of our lives that if we don't communicate, we can't survive.

When we talk of communication, there are many forms it can take. Communication can range from two individuals having a casual conversation, small groups working on a project, an individual giving a speech, to a reporter speaking to millions through the mass media. By learning about interpersonal communication, we can learn about each of these forms. Why? Because interpersonal communication is necessary in order to create relationships and function in the world. Julia Wood, in her text *Interpersonal Communication: Everyday Encounters,* discusses the important aspects of interpersonal communication.

## DEFINING INTERPERSONAL COMMUNICATION

To understand what interpersonal communication is, we can look to the Communication Continuum.

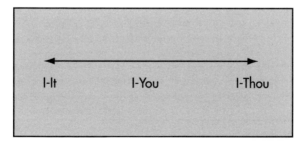

In general, interpersonal communication is communication that helps to establish and build relationships. The continuum illustrates the levels of interpersonal communication (Buber, 1970). I-it communication occurs when we perceive the other person as a non-being. Usually, we either do not communicate or have very limited communication at this level. For instance, we may pass homeless people on the street, ignoring their presence. Or if you have ever worked as a server in a restaurant, only to be treated as an entity to bring food and drinks, you have experienced I-it communication.

I-You communication is when we recognize the other person's existence, but the communication is somewhat impersonal in nature. With I-You communication, we will talk about casual topics, including the cliché of discussing the weather or the local sports team. At this level, the old saying usually applies, avoid talking about politics and religion. General chit-chat and safe topics are common here.

Finally, there is I-Thou communication. I-Thou occurs when we recognize another's individuality and hold that person in high regard. Most rare, communication here is deeply personal and involves a high level of trust between the individuals. When we feel as though we can talk about anything with someone, we have reached this level.

Our communication is not necessarily all one or the other among these levels. Instead, it can fall anywhere along the continuum. This model portrays the range of interpersonal communication in its many forms.

We can define interpersonal communication further by detailing more specific features. First, communication is an **on-going, systemic process.** This means that communication involves a system in which each part of the system affects and is affected by the other parts. The fact that communication is an on-going process means that communication is always happening.

Next interpersonal communication allows us to **build personal knowledge** within relationships. It is through talking with others that we begin to know who that person is and how to communicate with them. When we first meet someone, we are usually more formal than we are once we get to know them better. We learn if we can joke with our boss or discover a co-worker's personality quirks. This information will in turn shape how we feel about them and how we interact with them.

Finally, it is important to recognize that all communication has two levels of meaning. One, the **content level of meaning** is the literal meaning of our communication. There is also the **relationship level of meaning.** This level communicates information about the relationship between those interacting. Every time we communicate, we communicate each of these levels. For instance, an instructor may tell the class "Take out a pen, we're going to have a pop quiz." The content level of meaning is that the instructor wants the students to prepare for a quiz. But this statement also implies that the instructor has the power to control the class. This is the relationship level of meaning. There are three dimensions of the relationship level: power, liking and responsibility. Power refers to who has power within a relationship, or whether there is equal power. Liking is the level of positive or negative affection we have for another person. Responsiveness is how aware we are of others.

## Principles of Interpersonal Communication

We can further understand Interpersonal Communication by discussing the principles that affect our communication. First, **we cannot not communicate.** This means that we are always communicating, in some way at all times. The communication may be verbal or nonverbal, but communication is always occurring.

Another principle is that **communication is irreversible.** Have you ever said something you have regretted? We all have, and wished we could take it back or undo our words. Unfortunately, this isn't possible. Once done, communication cannot be undone. And the idea that **communication is a process** means that every piece of communication affects those that come afterward.

Next, **communication involves ethics.** Communication is a powerful force in our lives. It has the ability to affect ourselves, others, and the world around us in positive or negative ways. We have to make ethical decisions daily. If we make a derogatory joke about a particular group, it can be harmful to individuals from that group. What about lying? When is it wrong or right? Is it okay to tell our friend we like her haircut when we don't? Because communication impacts our lives in so many ways, we must be aware how it can affect us.

Finally, **effective communication can be learned.** No one is born a great communicator. We learn our communication skills just as we learn how to tie our shoes or learn world history. We may learn positive or negative behaviors along the way. Through our communication with our family and friends, as well as our personal experiences, we develop habits and styles that may or may not work for us. However, just as we learn a negative behavior, we can learn to improve our skills. In order to do so, we must cultivate knowledge of the specific forms of communication and the factors that affect them. Once learned, we can benefit our relationships, whether it involves family, friends or co-workers.

Photo courtesy of Photos.com

## Verbal Communication

Our words are extremely powerful. With our words we can express our feelings, insult someone, reminisce about the past, or philosophize. Verbal communication involves only our words. It is important to know that **all of our communication is symbolic.** The words we use are symbols to which we apply a meaning. Symbols are not intrinsically connected to the meanings we apply. This means that words can have different meanings given to them. This explains how the definition of words can change over time. For example, "cool" can refer to temperature, but has also come to refer to something we like. Symbols are also abstract. The abstract nature of language allows us to consider objects and ideas that are not immediate. We can talk about things such as love although we cannot physically see it. We can daydream and set goals for the future.

Another important factor of language is that our **words shape** how we see the world around us. Our use of language influences how we interpret people, objects and ideas. Our words are not neutral, they can have positive or negative connotation. Is your friend assertive or aggressive? Is your roommate organized or anal retentive? Each of these terms implies a different interpretation. This can be obvious when someone uses hate speech. Using language that is hateful toward a person or group can lead to an attitude of hate. This concept is the basis for the movement of political correctness. The idea is that if we use language that is inclusive and respectful, it will create a more positive attitude.

Finally, **verbal communication involves rules.** Researchers (Cronen, Pearce & Snavely, 1979; Pearce, Cronen & Conklin, 1979) have identified two types of rules. The first are regulative rules. These rules regulate interaction. They tell us who, where, when, how and about what we will communicate. It may be inappropriate to talk to your grandparents in the same manner in which you speak to your friends. We usually do not disclose personal information to complete strangers. The second types of rules are constitutive rules. These rules tell us what particular communication means. If someone speaks in a formal manner, they may be communicating professionalism. Complementing someone is a way to communicate that we like that person. Each of these is an example of constitutive rules.

## Nonverbal Communication

Nonverbal communication is every type of communication excluding words. It is estimated that around 70 to 90 percent of all of our communication is nonverbal. It includes our facial expressions, our style of dress, how we speak and more. Nonverbal communication is also **symbolic** and has meanings to which we apply meaning. Nonverbal communication is also perceived to be **more believable** than verbal communication. While not always correct, generally if someone says one thing and their nonverbal communication contradicts their words, we will believe the nonverbal communication more. While we often make a conscious attempt to control our nonverbals, there are often times that we are communicating even though we may not be aware of it. When we get dressed for classes in the morning, we are probably not trying to portray a specific image. However, people who see us will interpret our clothing in some way.

As we mentioned earlier, communication involves **rules.** Nonverbal communication also follows both regulative and constitutive rules. For instance, should we yell at our boss or stare at a stranger? What does it mean when a co-worker pats us on the back? We use rules to help us navigate the world of communication. We also discussed the idea that communication involves two levels of meaning. Nonverbal communication often helps to **establish the relationship level of meaning** in each of the three dimensions of power, liking and responsiveness. A manager with a higher level of power is more likely to enter the space of an employee. Our facial expressions or tone of voice can indicate like or dislike. Our eye contact may signal to someone we are listing to them. As you read through each type of nonverbal communication, consider how it may help communicate the three dimensions.

## *Types*

### *Artifacts:* Our Personal Belongings

The items we own communicate who we are to others. If someone sees you with your books for class, they may be able to infer your major or your interests. Studies have been done to determine how the types of car we drive says something about who we are. Sports cars denote an outgoing personality. Luxury sedans imply high standards and compact cars indicate an emphasis on logic and analysis.

### *Chronemics:* Our Use of Time

There are two approaches to our use of time. The monochronic use of time has a singular view and set structure. Polychronic use has much less structure. In the United States, we are monochromic. We place a high value on time and follow the clock very closely. In polychromic cultures, a meeting scheduled to meet at 9:00 a.m. may begin at 9:15 or 9:30, depending on when everyone arrives. In these cultures, time is not valued as highly.

### *Environmental Factors:* Our Surroundings

This includes the architecture, colors, temperature, sounds and smells of a setting. Each of these factors helps establish a mood and affects the communication. Businesses use environmental factors to control how customers will behave in their stores. Particular colors and odors have been found to enhance our buying patterns. Classrooms are designed to influence the interaction that occurs within them.

### *Haptics:* Our Touch

This includes everything from shaking hands to kissing. Cultural values influence how often touch occurs. For example, in general, women touch more than men. Touch can be used to show affection or display power over another. We may place a hand on someone's shoulder to provide comfort or to direct them in some way.

### *Kinesics:* Our Body Movements

Gestures, facial expressions, and eye contact are all included. We lean forward to show we are listening. Our facial expressions can communicate our emotions. People often rely on eye contact to determine if we are being honest or respectful. We can have either an open body position, arms down, head up, shoulders back, or closed, arms crossed, head down. An open body position is interpreted as a more open attitude and personality.

### *Physical Appearance:* How We Look Physically

Body styles are often the basis for our interpretation of a person's strengths and weaknesses. These interpretations are based on stereotypes, but we use them never the less. Physical appearance can also include hair styles, attractiveness, and body modification such as tattoos and piercings.

### *Paralanguage:* Everything That Is Vocal but Not Verbal

Laughter, crying, sighs, grunts, and yells are all examples. Paralanguage is also how we talk, such as our tone of voice, volume, and rate of speech. Paralanguage can provide the meaning for our words. If I say "you're such a jerk," the meaning can change based upon my tone of voice. I could be sincere or joking.

### *Proxemics:* Our Use of Space

In the United States, space can be separated into public distance (12 + feet), social distance (4 to 12 feet), personal space (18 inches to 4 feet), and intimate space (18 inches to contact). Proxemics also includes how we use the space around us. We often relate space with power. The size of someone's office can denote how much power they hold, from a shared cubicle to the huge corner office.

### Silence

We may think of silence as a lack of communication. However, silence can communicate many things. Silence can signal anger, shock confusion, thought, comfort or discomfort, and more.

> **ROLE PLAY ACTIVITY**
>
> Explore how nonverbal communication helps to establish the relationship level of meaning.
>
> **Power**
> A boss telling an employee that a project must be completed by the deadline.
>
> **Liking**
> First, two people who like one another passing each other on the street. Then, express dislike with the same scenario.
>
> **Responsiveness**
> One person discussing a problem with someone who is listening and interested. Then, the listener displaying a lack of responsiveness.
>
> Look for specific nonverbal behaviors that are used to communicate each of the dimensions.

# LISTENING

When we consider the importance of communicating effectively, we generally consider verbal and nonverbal behaviors. However, learning to listen well is just as important. About 60 percent of our communication is spent listening. We cannot be a good communicator if we are not a good listener. We spend more time listening than we do speaking, yet we often don't listen as well as we should.

## *Listening vs Hearing*

As you furiously toil to complete your term paper that is due the next day, someone enters the room. As they talk, you nod and answer quickly. Later,

Photo courtesy of Photos.com

paper completed, you realize you have no idea what was said. Has this scenario happened to you? Probably. Although we sometimes hear what is being said, we are not actually listening. Hearing is a physiological function that involves sound waves hitting our ear drums. We hear things all the time, it doesn't mean we are actually listening. There are constantly sounds occurring but we cannot take in everything we hear. Listening is a psychological process of taking in information, interpreting and responding. In order to listen effectively, we must concentrate and make an effort.

## *Types of Listening*

There are four types of listening and we actually listen differently depending on which type we are using.

> Appreciative: listening for enjoyment, such as listening to music.
> Empathic: listening to provide emotional support. We may listen to a friend discuss personal problems as a way to help them vent emotions.
> Comprehensive: listening to understand. As we sit in class and listen to a lecture, we are attempting to understand the information being presented.
> Critical—listening to evaluate. When we watch a political debate, we are trying to decide if we like an individual, if they are making good points, and if we agree with them.

## *Effective Listening*

There are steps we can take to become more effective listeners. This will allow us to become better communicators and can help us to remember information.

1. Get prepared to listen. In order to listen effectively, we must ready ourselves to be able to focus. This includes first getting rid of distractions: turn off the television or radio, clear desks of material that could divert our attention, or, if possible, move to an area free of other people. Being prepared also means we are mentally focused. We need to tell ourselves it's time to listen and clear our head of other thoughts.

2. Respond and stay involved. As we begin to listen, it can be easy to let our mind wander. However, we can take steps to help us stay focused. Nonverbals, such as body position and maintaining eye contact can keep our concentration on the individual speaking. Using minimal encouragers, including communication like uh-huh and go on, tells the speaking we are paying attention and encourages them to continue. Asking questions can also keep us involved.

Photo courtesy of Photos.com

3. Understanding. When listening, it is necessary to ensure we understand the information we have been told. To do this, we can ask questions for clarification. Paraphrasing is another method we can use. Paraphrasing is when we summarize and put the information into our own words. This allows us to check our perception and to make certain we accurately comprehend another's message.

4. Remembering. We only remember about half of what we hear, which doesn't bode very well for all the class lectures you attend. There are strategies we can use to help us improve these odds. Taking notes adds another dimension to our listening. It forces us to select the important pieces of information to record and gives us documentation to refer back to. Repeating the information, either aloud or internally, also helps the process of remembering.

By following this process, we can become better listeners. Once we improve our listening skills, we are on our way to becoming effective communicators.

## IMPORTANT COMMUNICATION PRACTICES

There are specific communication behaviors we can employ to improve our skills as communicators. Each of the following practices greatly impacts our ability to interact with others.

### Dual Perspective

Using **dual perspective** is the process of attempting to understand not only our own point of view, but that of others as well. This goes back to the adage of trying to walk a mile in someone else's shoes. We mentioned earlier the issue of noise, that we can never completely understand another's message as they meant it. What we can do is consider one's perspective, which will improve our chances to understand their message. Consider a couple is engaged in a conflict in which the man feels his girlfriend is spending too much time at work. He may interpret her behavior as disaffection and feel insecure about the relationship. She may think he doesn't understand how important her job is and feel he doesn't respect her needs. Without using dual perspective, it will be difficult for these individuals to resolve their conflict. However, if each makes the effort to listen to the other and understand how that person is feeling, it will be possible to comprehend their perspective. By doing this, the couple can focus on the issue and work to develop a solution which will satisfy each. It is only by using dual perspective that we can truly begin to know another person.

## *I-Language*

Emotions play an important role is communication. Every emotion we feel, happiness, dissatisfaction, envy, anger, or hurt, our emotions will impact how we interact with others. Research has shown that individuals with strong emotional communicative skills are more likely to have satisfying relationships and be successful at work. We must be able to express our emotions effectively to promote positive relationships. Often, we use You-language. This is when we place the responsibility for what we are feeling on someone else. We may say "you really hurt me." This is blaming the other person for our emotions and can create strong feelings of defensiveness within the relationship. Defensiveness often creates conflict and more negative feelings. The important factor here is that we alone control our emotions. No one can make us feel anything. By using **I-language,** we are accepting the responsibility for our emotions. Rather than "you hurt me," we say "I was really hurt because I felt you were ignoring me." This is not only more specific, but it will reduce the chance that the other person will feel attacked and become defensive. I-language can defuse conflict before it begins and promote mutual respect. This will help promote more open and effective communication.

## *Conflict Management Skills*

Conflict is a natural and inevitable part of every relationship. We think of conflict as negative, but it is simply the management of conflict that can create a negative situation. This belief can lead us to try to avoid conflict. However, this attempt does not rid us of conflict, it only prevents us from resolving it. Conflict can actually be a positive factor in relationships by allowing us to learn about ourselves, the other person, and the issues being discussed. We will look at the approaches to conflict and how we can improve our management skills.

There are four basic approaches to conflict. These refer to our attitude toward conflict and will affect how we deal with conflict. First is **lose-lose**. Someone with the lose-lose approach feels that conflict is negative and everyone loses when it occurs. Next is the **win-lose** approach. The win-lose attitude sees conflict as a competition in which one person wins at the expense of the other. Finally, there is the **win-win** approach. A person with the win-win attitude believes conflict can be resolved in a way that can satisfy everyone. Obviously, these approaches will impact how we communicate when conflict arises and will, in turn, affect the outcome. Each approach can be appropriate in different situations. Overall, however, one should work to maintain a win-win approach. Entering into conflict with this attitude provides the basis for more effective communication and more agreeable resolution for all involved.

There are specific things you can do to help resolve conflict in a positive manner.

### Stay Focused

One habit we often develop is called kitchen-sinking. This is a negative behavior that involves bringing up everything but the kitchen sink. Although the conflict usually involves one specific issue, we often bring other complaints or concerns into the conversation. The result is that we end up complaining back and forth and get off-track. We are not able to focus on the original issue and therefore will be unable to resolve it. This usually results in the original disagreement resurfacing in later conflicts. During a conflict, stay focused on the current disagreement. When other issues are named, set them aside to discuss later. You will be able to resolve the current conflict and then return to the other concerns that arose.

### Listen Effectively

When engaged in a conflict, we may feel the need to voice our own ideas and ignore those of the other person. However, if we do not listen, we will not be able to understand their ideas and concerns. Without this knowledge, we will not be able to work toward a positive resolution. By actively listening to the other person, we are able to establish common ground and begin to discover a solution. Remember that effective listening includes checking perception and using paraphrasing to ensure we understand their comments. Another benefit to good listening is that it communicates concern and respect for the other person. This can help promote positive emotions.

### Use Dual Perspective and I-language

As previously discussed, these two behaviors have many positive results. First, by practicing dual perspective, we are able to gain insight into the other person's perception which helps us understand the conflict more completely. Use of I-language prevents placing blame and creating defensiveness and negative feelings.

### Compromise

Work toward a resolution with which each person can be satisfied. No one will get everything they want, neither will they walk away empty-handed. This process will require some give and take, but when both individuals gain and sacrifice equal wants, both are likely to feel the result is one with which they are comfortable and contented. In this case, a win-win approach is likely to create a win-win situation. The result is that the conflict is resolved and the relationship can remain strong.

## *Satisfaction with Relationships*

Every type of relationship can benefit from this idea: **our words, thoughts, and emotions are interrelated.** Our words shape our thoughts and emotions; our thoughts affect our emotions and words; our emotions impact our words and thoughts. The key is that when one of these factors is positive, it has a positive effect on the others. If I pay a complement to someone, it will breed positive thoughts and emotions, which will result in more positive words. When one of these factors is negative, it can create a negative spiral. Being conscious of this fact, can help us become aware of something that may be creating problems in a relationship. It can also help us develop higher levels of satisfaction. This is one of the reasons that small, everyday behaviors can have such an impact of a relationship. Speak and behave in a positive manner and you will be more likely to create satisfactory relationships.

## *Culture affects communication*

Culture includes our beliefs, values and practices. These factors influence our communicative behaviors in multiple ways. In the next chapter, we will take a closer look at culture.

## REFERENCES

Buber, Martin. *I and Thou.* New York: Scribner, 1970.

Cronen, V., W.B. Pearce, and L. Snavely. "A Theory of Rule-Structure and types of episodes and a study of perceived enmeshment in undesired repetitive patterns." *Communication Yearbook, 3.* Ed. D. Nimmo. New Brunswick, NJ: Transaction, 1979.

Pearce, W.B., V.E. Cronen, and F. Conklin. "On what to look at when analyzing communication: A Hierarchical model of actors' meanings." *Communication,* 4 (1979): 195–220.

Wood, Julia. *Interpersonal Communication: Everyday Encounters, 4th Ed.* Belmont, CA: Thompson-Wadsworth, 2004.

# Chapter 9

## Communication Interculturally

*Culture is everything. Culture is the way we dress, the way we carry our heads, the way we walk, the way we tie our ties, it is not only the fact of writing books or building houses.* Aime Cesair

Photos courtesy of Photos.com

In the United States business world, we place a high value on straightforward, direct communication. When President George H.W. Bush went to Japan with Lee Iacocca to negotiate, he adhered to the American customs and made direct demands upon the Japanese businesses. The direct nature of the negotiations violated Japanese etiquette. In Japan making demands is interpreted as rude and a sign of ignorance or desperation. The misunderstanding surely harmed the negotiations and created a negative view of Americans among the Japanese.

Cultural misunderstandings happen quite frequently. Whether it involves international policy, business deals or casual conversations, the differences in our communication behaviors and values can create confusion, at best, or, at worst, insult and resentment.

What is your culture? What customs do you follow? What do you value? Have you ever experienced misunderstanding due to cultural differences? Often when we think of culture, we think of it as something that other people have. We're just "normal." Other people's different dress, religion, or practices come to mind to represent culture to us. However, it is important that we recognize not only others' culture but our own as well. It is our culture that dictates our daily behaviors and interactions as well as what we view as important in our lives.

These days, we often hear about the importance of diversity. It really is a small world, and it's continuously growing smaller. Just 50 years ago, most people grew up, had careers, and raised their families in one region. Now, we have increased mobility with more people than ever moving across the country and around the world with a growing global economy. Additionally, new technology allows us to communicate with individuals from every country from our own homes. Yet often our knowledge of other cultures is based solely on preconceptions and stereotypes. Regardless of your chosen career, from the arts to sciences to education, you will interact in a diverse world. It is increasingly essential that we learn about our own and other cultures in order to improve our communication skills.

## DEFINING CULTURE

Defining culture can be a difficult undertaking. There are countless approaches used by scholars in nearly every field. There are some commonalities however, and here we will use one definition developed by Clifford Geertz and interpreted by Gerry Philipsen in his book *Speaking Culturally*. The following definition incorporates the many various aspects of culture:

> *Culture is a socially constructed and historically transmitted pattern of symbols, meanings, premises and rules.*

## Culture Is Socially Constructed

To say that culture is socially constructed means that culture is created by society. This implies two things. First, culture is not individual. No man is an island, as the saying goes. Each of us exists within a structure that consists of our families, peers and society at large. Each of these impact our lives in many ways. Culture is not something we wake up one day and decide we have. Second, culture is created, not biological. Culture is not something we are born with. Culture is different from race or sex. A child born in Vietnam but adopted and raised by American parents will belong to the culture of the parents. Racially, the child is Vietnamese, but his or her culture will be American.

## Culture Is Historically Transmitted

Our culture is passed down through the generations. We learn our culture from our families, who learned it from theirs and so on. Some of the first things we learn as children are nonverbal behaviors. We discover quickly the meaning of someone's tone when speaking. Are they happy, mad? We begin making gestures to communicate our desires before we are able to speak. We wave hello and goodbye. Our verbal and nonverbal communication are the most basic aspects of our culture. Additionally, our parents teach us what is right and wrong, how we should behave and what is important in our lives.

Of course, this does not mean that culture always remains the same. Each generation brings revisions to their culture. Our views may change concerning what is acceptable. Women in the first half of the century were generally not allowed to wear pants. Only dresses were considered suitable. In the United States, this rule has obviously become less common. As times, events and society evolves, so does our culture.

## Culture Consists of Symbols, Meanings, Premises, and Rules

### Symbols and Meanings: The Golden Arches

*"Would you like fries with that?"*

In studies conducted around the world, researchers have looked for commonalities and differences in the symbols we use. One of the most commonly recognized symbols is McDonald's Golden Arches.

A **symbol,** simply stated, is anything that represents something else. A **meaning** is the definition we apply to the symbol. There may be some symbols that immediately come to mind when thinking culture. Each country's flag is an example. In the United States our flag has many meanings, from the colors and stars representing each state to the ideals of freedom and liberty. There are other symbols too, from symbols such as $, %, or @ to emotions increasingly used in email. These are most certainly cultural symbols but there are other symbols, perhaps less obvious but more integral

Language is one set of symbols that exists within each culture. Every word is simply a symbol that represents a particular meaning we have attached to that word and every culture has its own set of these symbols and meanings. If you have ever tried to talk with someone who does not speak the same language, you have experienced the differences of symbols. Even English is not the same around the world. The English spoken in Great Britain is not the same as American English. Some examples are below:

| England | America |
| --- | --- |
| Chips | French fries |
| Rubber | Eraser |
| Trolley | Shopping cart |
| Lift | Elevator |
| Flat | Apartment |
| Fag | Cigarette |
| Biscuit | Cookie |

You have probably even experienced verbal misunderstandings with someone you would consider to be of your own culture. As a transplant to the southern United States, I have had some confusing experiences of my own. Soon after I moved, I was asked by a native co-worker if I wanted something to drink. I replied I would like a Coke and was surprised when asked what kind. I quickly realized that "coke" was the term used to refer to any type of soda, while I used it specifically to refer to Coca-Cola. This was just the first of many misunderstandings.

Another system of symbols that exists within cultures is our nonverbal communication. Nonverbal symbols include everything from hand gestures and facial expressions to our clothing and status symbols. Again, each culture has its own set of nonverbal symbols and meanings they apply to those symbols. One student from China told the story of the first time her classmates waved to her as she passed them on her way to class. She explained she didn't know if they were asking her to come over, telling her to stay away, or trying to warn her of some danger. Within her culture, long-distance greetings were not the norm. Instead, it is customary to wait until you are face to face and can greet each other verbally.

Colors can also be symbolic. Within the American culture, brides often wear white to represent purity. In China, brides wear red as a symbol of long life and prosperity; white is used for death. Body language is symbolic as well. We nod our head to signal yes or shake our head to signal no. Eye contact is interpreted as a sign of respect and honesty. Yet both of these are also culturally-bound. Nodding can signal no and eye contact can be interpreted as disrespect. As you may have guessed by now, everything within a culture is symbolic and we provide meanings to each and every symbol.

## Premises Influence Our Culture

**Premises** are our beliefs of existence and of value. They are what we believe to be real and what we consider to be good or bad. In other words, our premises are our belief and value systems. One premise may be our belief of the existence of God. Most religions believe in the existence of God or a higher power, although they may use different names, or symbols, to refer to the higher power. Atheists do not hold this belief. For thousands of years, philosophers have studied and debated over premises. What is existence? What is real? All of these ideas fall under our premises.

Our values are also part of our premises. Cultures place value on different things. Within the American culture, family, education, success, health and money are all examples of our values. One area researchers often refer to is the concept of individual versus collectivist cultures. Individualistic cultures place the highest value on the individual person while collectivist cultures emphasize the importance of the family or group. The United States is an example of an individualistic culture while Japan is an example of a collectivist culture. These values impact our daily lives. For example, in Japan, it is common for multiple generations of a family to live together in one home. Caring for family members is considered to be a responsibility that is taken very seriously.

Our premises have an impact on all aspects of our culture. They influence the meanings we give to symbols and the rules we follow. For instance, if we value money and "stuff" we may interpret a Hummer as a powerful symbol of success. However, if we place a high value on the environment, we could interpret the same Hummer as a symbol of waste. In this sense, our premises are the basis of all the other facets of our culture.

## Every Culture Has Rules

**Rules** are prescriptions for how to act, in specific circumstance which carry some degree of force with a culture. In other words, there are particular behaviors that are acceptable in different situations. Rules carry force because there are repercussions if we do not follow the rules. The degree of force depends upon the importance of the rule and how extensive the repercussions are. Society's laws are examples of rules we must follow. If we do not, we may be fined or spend time in jail. Social rules are enforced in other ways. For instance, one specific circumstance in which we have rules to follow is in the library. The rules are numerous: we should be quiet, use the computer responsibly, check out our books, etc. If we talk too loudly, we could be the recipients of a dirty look or be asked to leave the library. If we leave with a book we haven't checked out, you could be charged with theft.

However, there are rules in everyday interactions as well. Consider **greeting** someone. Rules abound is this situation. First, how do we greet? Do we shake hands, bow, or give a kiss on each cheek? Within the American culture, we usually ask, "How are you?" What does this mean? Do we really want to know how that person is doing? Of course not. We want to hear "fine" or "good." This is a rule. If someone tells us how they are actually doing, we are quickly disinterested.

Another rule concerns **space.** Different cultures have different rules relating to our use of space. In the American culture, we like a lot of personal space. We feel very uncomfortable when someone stands or sits too close to us. This goes back to our premises. Individualistic cultures desire more space than do collectivist cultures. Another example of our premises influencing our rules can be seen in our funerals. Whether we view a funeral as a sedate time to mourn or an opportunity to celebrate the person's life is based on our beliefs and how we view death.

Often, we are not aware of the rules we follow within our culture. Usually, it takes a misunderstanding or violation before we realize a rule exists. We may not think about the rules of space until someone enters our personal space. When this occurs, the rule becomes abundantly clear. Learning to recognize rules may be difficult but it can help us to improve our abilities to communicate effectively-and without offending someone!

## SUBCULTURES

**Subcultures** can be defined as smaller social groups with their own symbols, meanings, premises, and rules. Subcultures exist within the context of a larger culture. You belong to many subcultures, though you may not realize it. We are able to move from one subculture to another, adjusting our communication as we go. This is a testament to our skills as communicators. However, we can improve our abilities when we recognize the intricacies of our subcultures.

Subcultures have some commonalities that often help to form or continue the social groups. First, subcultures often have a name that ties its members together. The

| EXAMPLES OF SUBCULTURES |
|---|
| Age |
| Gender |
| Religion |
| Occupation |
| Geographical region |
| Political affiliation |
| Major |
| Fraternities/sororities |
| Sexuality |
| Sports |
| Hobbies/interests |
| Families |

name may be official, as in the case of a fraternal organization, or an unofficial term such as "student." Subcultures also have a shared set of both visual and verbal symbols. Subcultures develop their own language and someone who is not a member of that subculture may be unable to understand the symbols. Do you remember when you first began college? Often, as beginning students, we are confused by the "college-ese" used among the college subculture. It takes us some time to learn the language. Visual symbols are also usually present within subcultures. Visual symbols allow us to recognize other members of the subculture. It may be the style of dress or a logo of a particular group. Finally, subcultures have shared values. Often it is the common values that unite or maintain a group. Some social clubs, for instance, highly value community service. Individuals who possess the same ideals may be drawn to join that club based upon the shared values.

There are millions of subcultures that exist around the world. Subcultures can be broken down into many classifications, some examples are given in the inset above. One set of subcultures to which everyone belongs is that of gender. Remember, culture is not biological. When discussing men and women, we are focusing not on sex, the biological differences between males and females, but on the cultural aspects of gender. Communication researcher Jonathan Gray created a commotion when he introduced the idea that men are from Mars and women are from Venus to the self-help world. While men and women inhabit the same world, there are certainly discrepancies between our cultures. One example is how we develop and maintain our relationships. Women develop closeness through dialogue, men through doing. Essentially, women are generally more verbal than men. When expressing closeness women may, for example, go to dinner and sit and talk with their friends. Men are more likely to talk less and do activities together, often referred to as male bonding, to accomplish the same. Neither method is better than the other, but the disparities can create misunderstandings in a relationship between a man and a woman. What do the words, "let's talk about us" mean to you?

---

**MEN'S GUIDE TO WOMEN'S ENGLISH**

It's your decision. = The correct decision should be clear by now.
Do you like this recipe? = It's easy to fix so get used to it.
I'll be ready in a minute. = Kick off your shoes and find a good game.
Is my butt fat? = Tell me I look good.
You're so . . . manly. = You need to shave and shower!

**WOMEN'S GUIDE TO MEN'S ENGLISH**

I'm hungry. = I'm hungry.
I'm tired. = I'm tired.
What's wrong? = I don't see why you are making a big deal about this.
Yes, I like your new hair cut. = I can't see any difference.
I like that one better (while shopping). = Just pick any dress and let's get out of here!

> **CULTURAL ACTIVITY**
>
> What do you have with you right now that is a symbol of subcultures to which you belong?
>
> Pick one item you have with you that expresses something about your culture. Within your group, discuss the meanings of these symbols.

## UNDERSTANDING CULTURE

*No culture can live if it attempts to be exclusive. Gandhi*

### Ethnocentrism

As we have seen, culture is a complicated system that permeates and impacts every part of our lives. Culture's importance dictates the necessity of studying and understanding how it affects our interaction. As previously mentioned, we often notice the cultural differences of others but rarely perceive our own. This can lead us to view different culture as Others. This can promote an alienation from those who we perceive as "different." In turn, the alienation can become dangerous.

**Ethnocentrism** occurs when the use our own culture as the standard by which to judge other cultures. We view our culture as the correct or normal way to believe and behave and any deviation from that is then considered incorrect or abnormal. This attitude is natural. As previously stated, we learn our culture. When our parents and families are teaching us, they often tell us "this is the right way to do it" or "no, you shouldn't behave that way." They teach us our symbols, meanings, premises and rules. So it is to be expected that even as adults we view beliefs and practices different from our own as inappropriate or even offensive. In the United States, a common example is the comment that in some countries they drive on "the wrong side of the road." Is it the wrong side or the opposite side? Many Americans follow the practice of love marriages, in which we chose our own partners, and disapprove of arranged marriages common in some cultures. Racist language is another, more dangerous, form of ethnocentrism. Any individual from every culture can hold this belief. I experienced this myself when, on a trip to Morocco, several women in our tour group wore shorts or pants. We were the recipients of many angry glares and under-the-breath comments. It was not appropriate for a woman to wear pants, let alone show her legs.

Ethnocentrism may be common, but it is also dangerous. Our views can move quickly from "that's weird" to "that's wrong" to "that needs to be stopped." When we don't respect a person's culture, we are not respecting that person. There are numerous instances of ethnocentrism and its negative effects throughout history. We see it with the Holocaust, in which eight million people were killed because they believed or behaved differently. We see it with religious radicals who feel it is moral to rid the world of those of another faith. We see it in cultural genocides still occurring today.

## *Cultural Relativism*

In order to avoid ethnocentrism, it is essential that we understand the people and cultures around us. **Cultural relativism** is the process of attempting to understand a culture on its own terms while withholding judgment. It is when we endeavor to comprehend the premises that underlie the rules and meanings of a culture. An example of this occurred in U.S. boarder schools that had large percentages of Mexican immigrant students. Teachers were frustrated that the Mexican-American students were not participating in class in the same manner as their Caucasian-American counterparts. After studying the issue, they soon discovered that within their collectivist culture, it was not appropriate to try to stand out over your peers. Therefore, competition and raising your hand to answer questions in class was considered rude. Once this factor was understood, teachers were able to adapt their methods in a way that benefited everyone. Both the Mexican-American and Caucasian students began to perform better and the teachers' frustration was eliminated. Cultural Relativism does not mean that we must accept or agree with another culture's beliefs and practices, it simply involves trying to understand the reasons behind them. By understanding and knowledge can limit the hatred and intolerance that is often bred through ethnocentrism.

## APPLYING OUR KNOWLEDGE

> *Culture is not just an ornament, it is the expression of a nation's character and at the same time it is a powerful instrument to mold character.* William Somerset Maughan

As we have seen, culture is not just an element of our lives, it is the foundation for how we perceive the world around us and how we interact with that world. Culture impacts our communication. In order to improve our skills and our ability to communicate effectively with those around us, we must be able to examine our own symbols and meanings, premises and rules. It is not until we accomplish this difficult task that we will have a true understanding of the world and of the diverse society within it.

Culture can be thought of as a pair of contact lenses. They are put into our eyes when we are born and shape everything we see and interpret. It is not until we can learn to remove those lenses that we can begin to understand our own culture as well as those of others.

# CREATE-A-CULTURE

Pick one item you have with you that expresses something about your culture. Within your group, discuss the meanings of these symbols. Then answer the following questions to create your own unique culture.

1. Where does your culture live?

2. What kind of clothing do you wear?

3. What types of food do you eat?

4. What type of shelter do you use?

5. How do you communicate with each other?

6. What natural features in your surroundings have influenced your development? How?

7. What do you do in your leisure time, or for entertainment? (Music, paintings, crafts, etc.)

8. Is there anything unique in your culture? (Ceremonies, religion, lifestyles, etc.)

9. Create a totem for your clan. (Totem: An animal, plant, or natural object serving among certain people as the emblem of a clan or family.)

10. What are the three most important rules in this culture?

11. What is the ONE rule, object, or idea from your real-life culture that you would want to leave behind?

12. What is the ONE rule, object, or idea from your real-life culture that you wouldn't want to do without?

# REFERENCES

Geertz, Clifford. *The Interpretation of Cultures: Selected Essays.* New York: Basic Books, 1973.

Philipsen, Gerry. *Speaking Culturally.* Albany: State University of New York Press, 1992.

# Chapter 10

## Communication and the Media

### Introduction

One thousand years ago, the world was stumbling through a period of time that has been called "The Dark Ages." During that time, the fountain of free thought and information had been—to some degree—dammed up by the Roman Catholic Church, which was the predominant church of Western Europe during that time. The "church"—which in today's world is seen by many as an institution of truth and enlightenment—had mysteriously led its flocks into the bondage of intellectual slavery and dependence.

Fortunately, that bondage was broken by two 15th century men who thirsted for truth. In about 1450 A.D., Johann Gutenberg (who is a forefather of today's computer geeks and nerds) made the first movable type printing press. In 1455, he printed his first book—The Gutenberg Bible. Twenty-eight years after Gutenberg printed his first Bible, Germany bore another native son whose ideas would revolutionize the church and the world. His name—Martin Luther. On Halloween of 1517, Luther nailed his 95 Theses to the church door at Wittenberg, accusing the Roman Catholic Church of multiple heresies. Many theologians believe this act was the beginning of the Protestant Reformation. The simple technology and profound ideas of these two men propelled the Western world into a new age that continues today—a world that thrives in using technology to pursue and communicate the ideas of truth and knowledge—and a world with an insatiable appetite for pleasure and to be entertained.

### The History of the Media (The History of the Entity That Made Britney Spears a Star)

#### Cavemen to Castles

On Thursday, September 12, 1940, four French teenagers, Marcel Ravidat; Jacques Marsal; Georges Agnel; and Simon Coencas, were roaming about on a hill overlooking the village of Montignac when they discovered a hole in the ground that had been opened by a fallen pine tree. They enlarged the hole and slipped through a narrow crevice. After tumbling down a pile of rocks, they discovered an entrance to a hidden

125

cave. They continued their adventure and went into the cave. What they discovered inside the cave was extraordinary. On the walls of the caves, they found paintings that had been drawn by prehistoric man possibly 15,000 years earlier. Their discovery of the Cave of Lascaux became one of the most renowned archaeological finds of the 20th century.

Located on the left bank of the river Vézère in Southern France, Lascaux is set a little apart from the traditional prehistoric sites that are located between Bugue and Moustier. The northern slopes of the Pyrenees and the western edges of the Massif Central in Southern France are famous for no fewer than 130 caves that were used by prehistoric man, dating back to 17,000 years ago. Some research at the Cave at Lascaux has placed its iconography at the beginning of the Magdalenian Age, or around 17,000 years ago. However, more research that included dating with Carbon 14, placed the age of cave drawings to a more recent period—around 15,000 years old. Whether these early cave drawings are 17,000 years old or 15,000 years old is of little relevance in the minds of the average college speech communication student. What should be important to them is the fact that the artists who painted the walls at Lascaux were making an attempt to express themselves. The Cave at Lascaux contains crude paintings of animals and humans. These painters were "telling their stories" in the most permanent fashion that they could at that time. In a sense, they were some of the world's first "newsmen." They were early forerunners of our modern day media.

As civilization progress, humans moved out of their cave dwellings and eventually into communal living of towns and cities. As they progressed, their ways of communication became more and more sophisticated. Around 4,000 years ago, the Egyptians developed papyrus—a new material on which they wrote and recorded the activities of their lives. As brilliant architects, they also used their monumental buildings as canvases to record their history.

Early Jewish civilization used stone and the skins of animals on which they wrote the accounts of their daily lives to preserve their history. This practice continued for thousands of years. Dramatic evidence of this practice came to international attention in the spring of 1947 when Bedouin goat-herders discovered caves located near the Dead Sea that contained jars filled with scrolls of early Jewish biblical scriptures. This discovery of the Dead Sea Scrolls opened many doors into the arenas of modern-day biblical scholarship and ancient Jewish history and culture. Between 1949 and 1956, 10 additional caves were found in the hills around Qumran that yielded several more scrolls, as well as thousands of fragments of scrolls dating from approximately 200 B.C. to 68 A.D. The scrolls found in the Qumran caves include early copies of biblical books, written in Aramaic and Hebrew; hymns, prayers, and other Jewish writings.

In Asia, the Chinese formed the letterpress as early as the sixth century and earthenware type in the 11th century. But, neither proved capable of mass production of printed materials. In 1040 A.D., Pi Sheng invented a printing process by using movable woodblocks. In Korea, movable copper type was invented as early as 1392. It was not until the mid-1400s that a machine was invented that was capable of producing mass quantities of printed materials. The machine was named in honor of its inventor—the Gutenberg printing press.

## Johann Gutenberg: Newspapers and Christianity Owe Him

Johann Gutenberg was born in 1397 A.D. to a wealthy family in Mainz, Germany. As a young man, he became a goldsmith and lived for some years in Strasbourg, Germany. He began experimenting with the idea of movable type around 1438 and formed a partnership with Andreas Dritzhen; but, that partnership quickly dissolved. He then partnered with Johann Fust, a wealthy German lawyer and goldsmith, who provided him with much needed financial backing. Gutenberg and Fust set up a printing press sometime between 1446 in 1450. Gutenberg's goal was to reproduce medieval liturgical manuscripts without losing their beauty of design or color. The printer's most famous masterpiece has been known by several different names: the *Gutenberg Bible;* the *Mazarin Bible;* and, in modern times, it is often referred to as the *42-line Bible,* so named for the number of lines in each printed column. Only 48 complete copies of *Gutenberg's Bible* are known to exist today. Two of the "perfect" copies are now held in European libraries, and one "perfect" copy is now held in the Library of Congress in Washington D.C. A copy is also held on permanent display in the Great Hall Library and is viewed by about one million people per year.

Photo courtesy of Library of Congress

## Newspapers: The Invention of Fish Wrap

Today in the United States, about 130 million people read at least one of about 1,500 newspapers that are printed on a daily basis. Weekly newspapers—many of which are free—reach an even larger circulation of about 200 million people a week. Although technology used to produce the newspaper has changed throughout the years, the editorial purpose of newspapers has remained the same for about 2,000 years—to keep the public informed. The earliest form of newspapers was called *acta dirua* or "daily acts." About 2,000 years ago, the Roman government posted hand written *acta dirua* documents in public places in order to keep its citizens informed.

More than one hundred years after Gutenberg introduced his printing press, Italian publishers in Venice, Italy, began selling actual news sheets in 1566 A.D. These documents are considered a rudimentary type of newspaper. In 1665, the first English newspaper, the *Oxford Gazette,* was published each week under the authority of the King of England. In 1702, London's *Daily Courant* became Britain's first daily newspaper.

In 1690, the first newspaper, *Public Occurrences,* was printed in the American Colonies. Not only does the *Public Occurrences* have the distinction as the "first newspaper in America," it also has the distinction of being the first newspaper to have been shut down by British authorities. After the newspaper printed a story about the French King's reported seduction of his daughter-in-law, the governor of Massachusetts closed the newspaper after only one day of operation.

Fourteen years later, the nation's second newspaper—the *Boston News-Letter*—began publication. This newspaper was printed under the watchful eye of government officials, who made sure nothing was printed that detracted or embarrassed the Massachusetts governor. Most of the content of the newspaper was dated stories, reprinted from the London Gazette. Local news items included brief notes about deaths; political appointments; ship arrivals; and stories about the activities of pirates and Indians.

Photo courtesy of Library of Congress

As "authorized" newspapers continued to appear in Colonial America, more and more publishers found themselves in trouble with British authorities. One of those publishers was Benjamin Franklin's brother, James Franklin, who published *The New-England Courant* in 1721. After being jailed for a month, upon his release, James was forbidden by British authorities to publish the *Courant,* or any similar paper. Undaunted, James turned over the publication of his newspaper to his brother, Benjamin, who wrote for the newspaper using the pseudonym, Silence Dogwood. Benjamin's writing talent was evident, and his work became popular. But, as newspaper journalists' stories often do, Benjamin's stories upset some people—even to the point that his life was threatened. Later, Benjamin Franklin became publisher of the *Pennsylvania Gazette* and the owner of a chain of newspapers. He also published *Poor Richard's Almanack,* which was one of the first magazines in America.

On July 4, 1776, the American colonies declared their independence from Great Britain and established the United States. Shortly thereafter, the early leaders of the United States created the U.S. Constitution. Two of the most important rights that was guaranteed by the Constitution were the rights of freedom of speech and freedom of assembly. These rights guarantee the freedom for all Americans to assemble peacefully and to be able to speak freely and, if a person chooses to do so, to criticize the American government and its leaders. The Constitution also guarantees the rights of a free press. Today, these rights are considered almost sacred in the United States.

The growth of the newspaper industry exploded in the 19th century. The mid-1800s was known as the "Penny Press" era in American journalism. It was during this time that the Associated Press (AP) was formed (1846). The Associated Press, which is still alive and well today, is a collective news service through which newspaper affiliates share news stories and information with other affiliates. The telegraph was used to share the first AP stories. In 1851, *The New York Times* was founded by Henry J. Raymond. Raymond created the leading newspaper in the country by urging his writers to do in-depth reporting and serious-minded editorials. Today, *The Times* continues to be one of the leaders in American journalism,

During the American Civil War (1860—1865), major newspapers hired war correspondents to cover the bloody conflict. The use of the telegraphic wire services supplied newspapers with timely coverage of stories and spurred newspaper circulation and readership. Photographer

Photo courtesy of Photos.com

*Photo courtesy of Library of Congress*

Mathew Brady became the first wartime photographer. His sometimes graphic images are still used in publications today and are a grim reminder of the carnage and brutality of war.

During the 20th century, the newspaper industry continued to grow and competition among news organizations thrived. Newspaper reporters covered three major wars, World War I; the bombing of Pearl Harbor and the horrors of World War II; and the Vietnam War; the 1929 Stock Market Crash; the depression of the 1930s; the Civil Rights movement; the assassinations of President John F. Kennedy; Dr. Martin Luther King; Malcolm X; and Senator Robert Kennedy; man's first steps on the moon; the resignation of President Richard Nixon; Jimmy Carter's rise to power from a peanut farmer to President of the United States; the tearing down of the Berlin Wall; the colorful presidency of "The Great Communicator" Ronald Reagan; and the impeachment proceeding against President Bill Clinton. On January 1, 2000, newspapers around the world were filled with stories of the dawning of a new millennium, an event that only occurs once in a thousand years. On September 12, 2001, newspaper headlines throughout the world expressed shock and dismay of the attack of the United States and mourned the devastation and deaths of innocent people who worked at the World Trade Center and the Pentagon and those who died when the hijacked plane crashed in a Pennsylvania field.

## THE CAMERA: PICTURE THIS!

The word "photography" is derived from the Greek words photos (light) and graphein (to draw). Sir John F. W. Herschel, a scientist, first used the term in 1839. Photography is a method of recording images on a sensitive material by the action of light. As early as 330 B.C., Aristotle recognized some of the principles of photography. In his work, *Problems*, the great Greek philosopher questioned how the sun makes a circular image when it shines through a square hole. This concept, which in 1604 was identified by Johannes Kepler as Camera Obscura, was the direct forerunner of the camera. In 1609, Kepler suggested that the image projected by a Camera Obscura could be improved by using a lens.

During the Middle Ages, Alhazen Ibn Al-Haytham, who live about 1000 A.D. and who was a leading authority on optics, invented the pinhole camera. About 1600 A.D., Della Porta, a European, reinvented the pinhole camera. Louis-Jacques-Mandé Daguerre, the inventor of the first practical process of photography, was a professional scene painter for the opera. In the 1820s, Daguerre experimented and studied the effects of light upon translucent paintings. He partnered with Joseph Nicéphore Niépce in 1829 to improve the process that Niépce had developed in taking the first permanent photograph in 1826–1827. After experimenting for several years, Daguerre developed a more effective method of photography and named it after himself—the daguerreotype. The daguerreotype gained popularity quickly; by 1850, there were more than 70 daguerreotype studios in New York City.

George Eastman, who was born in 1854, was an American inventor and philanthropist, who played a leading role in transforming photography from an expensive hobby into an inexpensive and popular pastime. Eastman patented the first film in roll form in 1884. Four years later, he perfected the Kodak camera. It was the first camera designed specifically for roll film. He established the Eastman Kodak Company, at Rochester, New York. The company was one of the first to mass-produce standardized photography equipment and to manufacture the flexible transparent film. Eastman was associated with the company in an executive and administrative capacity until his death in 1932 and contributed much to the development of its notable research facilities.

## THE TELEPHONE: HONEY, MA BELL'S CALLING!

In the 1870s, two inventors Alexander Graham Bell and Elisha Gray both independently designed electronic devices that could transmit speech. Both men carried their respective designs to the patent office within hours of each other, Bell arrive at the patent office first and patented his telephone. Gray and Bell entered into a legal battle; Bell won. Bell's success with the telephone came as a direct result of his attempts to improve the telegraph. Bell's experimentation with electrical signals of the telegraph led to his invention of the telephone and the first electrically transmitted speech sounds. Speaking through his new invention to Thomas Watson, his assistant who was in the next room, Bell spoke the

Photo courtesy of Library of Congress

famous first words uttered on a telephone: "Mr. Watson—come here. I want to see you." Today, the telephone helps individuals throughout the world to connect with others. Throughout the world, trillions of dollars worth of business is conducted through telephone connections each year. Certainly, the telephone has proven to be one of mankind's inventions that has had a dramatic effect upon the world.

## THE RADIO: TURN YOUR RADIO ON

There is an old gospel song that has been recorded by many artists—most notably country music singer/comedian Ray Stevens—titled "Turn Your Radio On"—that encourages individuals to "turn your radio on; and listen to the music in the air," in order to hear the message of salvation. For almost one hundred years, people throughout the world have been "turning on" radios to hear varied messages and a host of different kinds of music. These radios have been in the form of many different shapes and sizes. Whether listening to President Franklin D. Roosevelt's "Fireside Chats" (1930s–1940s); or listening to the *Grand Ole Opry*—which is the longest running live radio show—while sitting on a rustic front porch in the Tennessee mountains (1920s—present); or listening to the soothing opera music of National Public Radio on a big stereo unit in their homes; or listening to the blaring beat of a favorite rapper while driving in their cars, Americans have enjoyed the companionship and convenience of the radio.

Without getting into highly technical jargon or explanations, the basic principle of radio transmission deals with sending and receiving electrical impulses through the airwaves. Throughout the 19th and 20th centuries, many brilliant thinkers and inventors contributed ideas and theories that led to the invention of the radio. One of those contributors was Samuel F.B. Morse who, in 1844, sent the message—"What hath God wrought!"—through his invention—the Telegraph. Using his wired Telegraph and special electronic language, the Morse Code, Morse was able to create the first long distance, instant communication system the world had known.

Twenty-one years later in 1865, Dr. Mahlon Loomis, a Washington, D.C. dentist, developed a method of sending and receiving signals by using the atmosphere of the Earth. The dentist/inventor sent the first wireless signals between two mountains in Virginia by attaching two kites, which were being flown 18 miles apart, to closed copper wires. The wires, which were buried into the ground, transmitted the signals using the Earth as its own conductor. On July 30, 1872, the U.S. government granted Loomis a patent for a form of wireless communication. One year later, Loomis incorporated his new business, the Loomis Aerial Telegraphy Company.

A few years later in 1887, Heinrich Hertz, while studying the data of a fellow scientist, detected and produced the first radio waves. While conducting an experiment with a crude transmitter and receiver, Hertz's discovered that the electrical sparks—or radio waves—traveled between the transmitter and receiver at the same rate as the speed of light—186,000 miles per second. Hertz's work was influential and was studied by other scientist, including Guglielmo Marconi, who many credit with the invention of the radio.

Even as a boy, Marconi, who was born April 25, 1875 in Bologna, Italy, had a keen interest in electrical and physical science. In 1895 he set up a laboratory at his father's estate in Ponecchio and conducted many scientific experiments with electricity. He eventually was successful in sending wireless signals over a distance of one and a half miles. In 1896 Marconi took his apparatus to England in 1896, where, later that year, he was granted the world's first patent for a wireless telegraphy system. He formed the Wireless Telegraph & Signal Company Limited in July, 1897, and renamed the company Marconi's Wireless Telegraph Company Limited a few years later. In 1899, he established wireless communication between England and France across the English Channel. In 1900, he received a patent for "tuned or syntonic telegraphy" and, one year later transmitted his first wireless signal across the Atlantic between St. John's Newfoundland, and Poldhu, Cornwall. In conducting the 2,100 mile transmission, Marconi proved that wireless waves were not affected by the curvature of the Earth. In 1907, Marconi perfected his transatlantic wireless system. He formed a company that offered commercial service between Clifden, Ireland, and Glace Bay, Nova Scotia. In 1909, he was awarded a Nobel Prize for his work in physics.

During World War I, the United States government forced Marconi's American company to merge with General Electric and some other American companies to form RCA. The move was forced by the government in order to avoid foreign control in the wireless properties used by the U.S. military. With the move, Marconi's influence in wireless communication in the United States was weakened. However, in Britain, Marconi's companies were instrumental in establishing public radio broadcasting and the company that eventually became the BBC—British Broadcasting Corporation. After making many significant contributions to the development of radio, Marconi died in 1937 of heart failure.

During the first half of the 20th century, radio was a dominant force in the dissemination of pertinent information and in the entertainment industry, especially in the development of the music recording industry. However, with the coming of age of television in the mid-1950s, radio began to lose its influence and popularity. Today, many radio observers believe that the radio broadcaster industry is struggling in the fast-paced, competitive world for advertising dollars. Many observers also believe that radio broadcasters will survive according to how quickly and effectively they adjust to the ever-changing world of technology.

## THE TELEVISION: A TUBE FOR BOOBS

Can you imagine living in a world without a television set? Many people long for "the good old days" when our lives were not filled with countless advertising images; mindless television programming; obnoxious "news" commentators; violent, graphic images of war depicted by television cameras; digitally-altered censoring of nudity (Howard Stern's program on the E Network); and many other objectionable ideas and programs presented on **their** television screens. The key word is "their."

Although many complain about television programming, most Americans believe they need a television set as part of the landscape of their domain. Statistics from the U.S. Census Bureau support this statement. According to the U.S. Census website, in 2001, there were 248 million television sets in American households with 98.2 percent of the households having at least one television set. This figure represents a healthy increase compared to the number of the television sets in U.S. homes in 1960 when 87.3 percent had at least one television set. Also, in 2001, there were an average of 2.4 television sets per home in the United States.

In their studies, the U.S. Census projected that in 2004, the average adult—18 years old and older—would spend 1,669 hours watching television. This is the equivalent of about 70 days. In 2002 statistics, it was found that 94.3 percent of people over 18 years old watched television during the spring of that year. It was found that older Americans—age 65 and older—were more likely to watch television on a more regular basis than any other group. The parents or guardians of 92 percent of children between the ages of six years old to 11 years old who watched television imposed at least one rule for watching TV. These restrictions included the type of program the children could watch; the number of hours they could watch; and how early or late they could watch television. The percentage of restrictions placed on children ages 12 to 17 dropped to 73 percent. In 2001, there were 1,937 television broadcasting networks and stations in the United States. According to Census 2000, 31,235 individuals worked behind the scenes as motion picture, television and video camera operators and editors. In 2001, there were approximately 245,000 employees working for 6,692 cable TV networks and program distribution firms in the United States. The annual payroll for these employees was $11.7 billion.

## Pass the V-Chips, Please!

With the freedoms that Americans enjoy, there comes conflict. Because there are so many different viewpoints and legal expressions of freedom in the United States, the government often finds itself in the delicate position of protecting the rights of individuals to freely express themselves while also protecting the rights of those who are offended by another's free expression. The Federal Communication Commission (FCC) often finds itself performing such a balancing act. In an effort to regulate and strengthen parental control of the television broadcast industry, President Bill Clinton signed the Telecommunications Act of 1996. In Section 551 of the act, Congress allowed the broadcasting industry to have an opportunity to create and establish a voluntary rating system that would rate programming that contained violent, sexual or any other material that parents would determine to be inappropriate. The broadcast industry, consisting of the National Association of Broadcasters, the Motion Picture Association of America and the National Cable Television Association, created the rating system, also known as "TV Parental Guidelines." For the first 15 seconds of a rated program, these ratings are displayed on the television screen and, in conjunction with the V-Chip, permit parents to block programming they determine to be inappropriate. To enforce the act, the FCC adopted rules that required television manufacturers to include the V-Chip on all television sets which were 13 inches or larger. The mandate went into effect on January 1, 2000.

## "The Power for Good" Factor

Even its most vocal critics can't deny the potential for good that television can produce. Certainly, the day we know simply as 9/11 was not a good day. But, Americans—and the world—were able to watch the events unfold before our eyes by watching television. Although we were disturbed by the events that we saw occur, it empowered us to make decisions concerning the matter for ourselves. During the aftermath of the attack, we were able to hear the pleas for help from the victims and act accordingly. We were able to see and hear the stories of true heroes who had died while saving many others' lives. We saw an outpouring of love and compassion throughout the country for the families of the victims of 9/11. We saw these things through the intimacy and immediacy of television.

Television can be a powerful force for good in our society. It serves as companionship for millions of individuals. It offers varied entertainment programs for the masses. It provides us with on-the-spot coverage of events as they occur. We can see the event occur through the "eyes" of a camera. All these aspects are important. But, perhaps most important of all, it helps us record and preserve the stories of our lives for future generations. In a sense, television is our modern-day Cave of Lascaux, documenting through pictures and sound the stories of our daily lives.

## Media Madness and U

"So," U ask yourself. "What does the media have to do with U and the fact that are stuck in a college speech class?" The answer is: EVERYTHING! Everyday, your life is influenced by the media. The "Powers Who Are" in the media sees U as a consumer. They know that U must have timely, accurate information to make the choices and decisions U must make. They know U. They study U. They understand U—often better than U understand yourself. Your concerns are their concerns. U reflect who they are. Ultimately, your story becomes their story.

### References

www.northwinds.net
www.nobelprize.org
http://lilt.ilstu.edu
www.usc.edu
www.otal.umd.edu
www.culture.gouv.fr
www.internetcampus.com
www.memory.loc.gov
http://inventors.about.com
www.fcc.gov/vchip
www.census.gov

*Communication Journeys* by Stuart Lenig, Kendall/Hunt Publishing Company

# Chapter 11
## Communication and Popular Culture

### POPULAR CULTURE

#### 1900–1940: The Culture Industry: Adorno and Horkheimer

Popular culture has an enormous influence over what we speak and how we see the world. The concept of a **self-conscious popular culture** is relatively new. Theodore Adorno began speaking of it in scathing terms in the 1930s due to the negative influence Hitler was having over German culture. In America, the more benign figure of Franklin Roosevelt presided over American culture but not in a harsh or dictatorial way. FDR used the radio to talk to people. During a depression there wasn't much he could do to make people do things unless they agreed with him, and most of his weekly messages provided support and faith messages for all Americans to help themselves and their country.

Adorno and his colleague Horkheimer were German Jews and they had seen Hitler's tyranny first hand. They argued that Hitler and Josef Goebbels had hijacked society with a series of masterful **propaganda** images that rapidly transformed the way the German populace saw the world. Adorno and Horkheimer called this propaganda machine, **the culture industry.** They literally believed that **powerful people could make or manufacture culture to say whatever they wanted.** If in 1932, Germans saw Jews as citizens, but 1935, they perceived them as an alien menace. Such was the power and terror of propaganda that it could remake a person's mind, reprogram their thinking, and condition people to believe the unthinkable. In the case of Nazi Germany the unthinkable was genocide, the extermination of a group of people that were thought to be less than citizens, and perhaps less than human. These ideas have not died. In Somalia in the early nineties, warlords sought out certain minority groups or competing tribesmen and had them exterminated as less than human. In Bosnia in the area formerly known as Yugoslavia, civil war erupted in the middle nineties and many serbs in the region know as Serbia began to believe that their former countrymen in the region known as Bosnia-Herzegovina were non-human vermin fit only for eradication. There was a genocidal war fought in the region with Serbs seeking to murder and destroy Bosnian society. The United Nations and General Wesley

Clark were ordered in to restore the peace and end the fighting. They did and it did.

But Adorno and Horkheimer's fear of culture industry persisted. When the two sociologists and scholars immigrated to the United States to avoid death in German they were horrified by what they saw as an **American culture industry.** This was not a propaganda war machine to kill people but in showing pictures of attractive Hollywood movie stars it was just as powerful and just as dangerous. Adorno argued that the images of Clark Gable, Frank Sinatra, and Marilyn Monroe could have an equally detrimental effect on people's thinking. They could begin to **believe that whatever they saw in film or in music or in the press was a reality,** including commercial messages, perhaps the most insidious tools of the culture industry. Adorno and his fellow sociologists feared the enormous power and influence of the popular media as much has they loved it and watched it themselves. Their warning was simple. Watch, but always be vigilant and beware of being seduced by ideas that seem charming and flattering but could have long term consequences for society

## THE SELLING OF CIGARETTES

Photo courtesy of Library of Congress

In the **16th century tobacco** was discovered in the **New World** and imported back to England and the continent by **Sir Walter Raleigh** and others. Smoking of pipes and cigars became very fashionable. It provided a sense of social class and it provided a sense of portable heat and warmth in the drafty and ill heated rooms of renaissance castles. Of course, at the time, most people were unconcerned about the health effects. After all, most people who were lucky enough to have fires in the homes to keep them warm had to endure choking smokes. It is thought that prior to smoking thousands may have died from passive and continual smoke inhalation. However, over time people recognized that smoking was likely producing health risks. It certainly produced fire risks. In Shakespeare's day, his famous theatre, **The Globe** was burned to the ground not once but three times on account of fire.

But for over two hundred years smoking was largely the province and the disease of males. While women were 'protected' from manly pursuits they were also protected from manly vices such as drinking, whoring and most assuredly smoking. Not only was smoking thought to be unwomanly it was thought to be a symbol of masculine power. Further the idea of a cigar or pipe dangling from a woman's mouth was thought to be quite ugly and unattractive. But in the late nineteenth century, the advent of mass market advertising began to change this perception. **Women's magazines** were promoted to teach women the feminine arts of home keeping and housework. Not unrelated were a series of new household products that were being marketed to aid women in their toil at home. Needless to say, such magazines, and such ads for kitchen and bath aids were clearly indicative of Adorno's culture industry. As the industrial revolution was rising and providing more wealth, affluence, education and free time, the hegemonic power of men trying to control women was slipping. Ibsen had written *A Doll's House,* Shaw had written the shocking story of an ex-prostitute, *Mrs. Warren's Profession,* and Zola had placed a woman as the central murderer and amoral figure at the center of *Therese Raquin.* Women were in the news and on the move and not in a way that men liked. In fact they feared their growing power. The magazines that had been created to bind women tighter to the home were now marketing to their beauty and ego needs. Women were finding group methods to assert domestic authority. Then, a clever fledgling tobacco industry toyed with another means to harness women in a leisure activity that would give them the appearance of sophistication and freedom, but would enslave them to tobacco and keep them as objectives posed for men's enjoyment. They created a new method to deliver nicotine (one of the world's most powerful addictive substances) and tobacco in a package that would look attractive on a woman....**the cigarette.** The triumph of the cigarette was its **packaging.** The white box looked elegant like something found on a ladies' vanity table. The cigarettes themselves were **thin and long** not short and stubby or coarse and brown like pipes, cigars, and pipe tobacco. The cigarette could be **held gently** in the hand and released from the mouth to give a framing effect to the face suitable for **photographs** and not distracting from female beauty. In fact the cigarette could be used to **extend the line** of the arm. Women's magazines lauded the cigarette as a coming of age, a liberation and a breath of freedom. Women in society, in film, on stage, and in musical realms adopted the new mode of smoking. **Smoking** became identified with the tough talking, violent, aggressive female power of Jean Harlow, Betty Davis and Joan Crawford. All became successful and energetic stars and all smoked prominently to show their new stature in American society.

## YOUTH CULTURE

Youth culture began a long rebellion against adult powers in the 50s with the outbreak of **Elvis** and the new form of rock music. This form continued and escalated into the well-organized youth culture of the sixties with its own cars, music, fashion styles, press and media, and vision of the world. This was the generation of peace and love. It changed talk from a highly formalized discussion to the arguments and rhetoric of rebellion. Che Guavara, Castro, Hoh Chi Mihn, and Mao became counter-cultural figures which horrified the young Republican parents that elected Nixon in 1968.

## TELEVISION TALK

Throughout, television's power escalated with talk shows, the *Tonight Show,* Phil Donahue, Merv Griffin, Mike Douglas, and a host of others either entertaining, sedating or angering American viewers. Phil Donahue gets credit for making female relationship talk the root subject of his investigative journalistic talk show. Finally in the nineties, Oprah Winfrey transformed talk television to be a medium for feelings and expression over thought and intellectual matters. So successful was Oprah at this revolution that even she attempted to move back to intellectual talk through her book club, her goal to re-civilize the talk of talk shows and themes presented on practical and positive issues. Viewers went right with her moral and ethical crusade. President Bill Clinton watched the transformation of American talk and succeeded to win people's hearts with his kind and empathetic speaking style.

### ORIENTALIZING AMERICAN POP CULTURE

The way we communicate as a culture is often conditioned by our exposure to our culture and often to the new cultures that we encounter. In the later twentieth century, we have been exposed to Asian cultures more and more. One critic called the late twentieth century, the Pacific rim era, the time of Pacific rim cultures. This means that in the dawning twenty-first century, the Pacific Rim cultures will be prominent to our culture. Noted Middle Eastern Palestine critic, **Edward Said,** proposed a theory about the relationship between Western and Eastern cultures. He argued that the West colonized the East as its colony and that the West never could see the East as anything other than a colony, something it owned. Said called this relationship **Orientalism,** the conception that the West only sees in the East what it wants to see. To Said, the West always saw the East as strange, primitive, exotic, and lesser. These were ways that the West psychologically controlled the East. It made itself feel comfortable by making the 'other' feel inferior. Today, that image of the East as an inferior part of the world is rapidly changing as the East rivals the West in its industry and its technological advancement. Today many computer industry jobs are moving to India. Many of the world's best cars are produced in Japan and Korea. Japan dominates the world in camera and electronic products. China now sells more products to Walmart, America's largest retailer, than any American corporation.

However, economic relationships do not alone make cultures complimentary. The cultures have to interact on a number of levels. America's interaction with Asia in a heavy and systemic way began with pearl Harbor. After five years of desperate war with Japan, the United States dropped Atom bombs on Hiroshima and Nagasaki in 1945. The resulting devastation demanded the United States take a strong and benevolent hand in rebuilding the country. More than any single figure, **General Douglas MacArthur** shaped the content on modern Japan making it a representative democracy based on an American capitalistic system. Japan championed capitalistic aesthetics and worshipped American popular culture. Their film industry studied America's films and **Akira Kurasawa** made a series of Samurai, action, and drama films based on Shakespeare and American

Photo courtesy of Library of Congress

westerns (***Throne of Blood, Rashomon, Seven Samurai***). These films became internationally famous and spawned an international audience for Japanese films and made Japanese culture less remote and mysterious.

The Japanese film industry also explored American genres such as horror movies. In ***Godzilla,*** the Japanese film industry responded to the horrors of nuclear war and nuclear proliferation. With added footage featuring American actors the film beget a series of films featuring an actor in a rubber suit repeatedly stomping a model of Tokyo. Most Americans did not take the Godzilla films seriously and in fact Japanese horror films were seen as low culture for several generations. But in recent years, Godzilla has been re-released minus the American footage and the original film is much darker. Godzilla is killed by a scientist who feels guilty for having created the monster through countless nuclear experiments. In the end, the scientist kills himself and the monster.

America saw Asian culture through books. In the fifties beat writer **Jack Kerouac** wrote ***Darma Bums, On the Road*** and other novels the infused Zen Buddhist principles in American themes. Kerouac's beautiful drifters may have seemed like California hippies, but his books had strong themes and philosophies borrowed from Asian cultures. In the seventies, **Robert Pirsig's *Zen* and *The Art of Motorcycle Maintenance*** tells the story of a man seeking to regain his life by travel, working on a motorcycle and deep meditation inspired by Buddhist methods. In colleges across the nation, the hippie movement made the Tao te Ching required bedside reading for many young college students. The inroads made by Asian auto makers began to impact the American auto industry and by 1975, Toyota Landcruisers and Corollas began to challenge the Ford and Chevys that had dominated American roads for fifty years. In academic circles, professor **Alan Watts** wrote a series of popular books including the best selling ***The Way of Zen*** that popularized Asian philosophies and suggested that western culture could benefit from seeing things from an Asian perspective.

The economic power of the new Asian culture was also reflected in the troubling news of the war in **Vietnam.** Raging since the early sixties, the Americans saw the small country of Vietnam and the rebel insurgents as a tiny police action. However, Ho Chi Mein's warriors were battle trained from a twenty year war against French imperialism and they weren't afraid of young and untrained American troops. In the next ten years, the Viet Cong were dubbed **King Cong** by American soldiers and over 40,000 American troops perished in the conflict, inflicting the first military defeat on American forces in the country's history. However, the brutal war provided another dark reason to respect the power of Asia.

The begrudging respect for Asian military prowess was found in the new interest in Asian Hong Kong kung fu movies. Most popular were the films featuring Chinese actor, **Bruce Lee**. He became famous in the Green hornet American television series where he played the Hornet's martial arts' aid, Kato. In *Fists of Fury* and *Enter the Dragon,* Lee became an international star. On television, the program *Kung Fu* featured David Carradine portraying a Chinese Kung Fu monk who journeyed across the American West during the late nineteenth century to become a chanting, fighting, Buddhist styled foil to American blustering, gun-slinging racism. In every episode, Kung Fu's Carradine preached peaceful coexistence with man and nature, but ultimately had to violently confront American racism and prejudice. The show mirrored American's attitudes of superiority towards Asia. The program was a minor cult hit which has been variously revived.

In the eighties, director Ron Howard scored a hit with his film, *Gung Ho* that starred Michael Keaton in a comedy where Japanese auto manufacturers were willing to take a chance on a decaying American industrial town and workers to make their new Asian car in this country. Today foreign investment in American workers is no laughing matter and means serious jobs. Hong Kong action director, **John Woo** became influential through a series of fast paced action movies starting with *The Killer, Hard-Boiled* and *A Better Tomorrow.* The director moved to the U.S. and became popular for films such as *Face Off, Mission Impossible II* and **Broken Arrow**.

Today, Japanese anime animation influences programming on America's **Cartoon Network.** Cartoon Network has featured *Yui Gui Oh, Cowboy Bebop* and *Vampire Hunter D.* American animations such as *Teen Titans* and *Samurai Jack* are deeply infused with Japanese graphic techniques and aspects of Asian culture. Most notably, Jim Lee and other artists have begun to pioneer a new way of drawing American icons such as *Superman.* In recent years, our national comic book hero has begun to long extremely Asiatic with eyes and body features that make him look like a hybrid of Western and Asian genetic features. This may reflect new science that suggests that our American ancestors may have arrived from Asia across the Bearing Straight crossing from Asia to Alaska across a land mass that once connected the two continents.

In any case, the persistent and increasing communication between Asia and the U.S. as economic partners and competitors is only bound to increase in the coming years. The deeper communication between these cultures will produce new levels of communication and may illustrate new levels of understanding and new ways of seeing the world. This might result in more interest in Asian business, Asian religion, and Asian governmental structures. Aside from this, cultural exchange is already thriving and rather than finding enemies in Asia, we might find our American vision of the 'Oriental' evolving into a more truthful and full portrayal of another group of the world's people.

## CARTOON TALK: SIMPSONS, BEVIS, AND SOUTH PARK

Cartoons began to influence children in a larger manner. They were no longer blocks of programming but now whole channels of entertainment that relegated kid speech to a kid ghetto of phrases, thoughts, ideas, needs, and consumer generated gratifications. In the nineties, **The Simpsons** dictated a series of catchphrases to American youth. "Don't have a cow, man," "Cowabunga," and "release the hounds," became common place expressions. MTV's experiments with animation allowed Mike Judge's crude and delightful Bevis and Butthead to rule the airwaves for several years. Butthead's repetitive moronic laughter and derisive lines like, "Bevis, you're never gonna' score," kept MTV's target demographic of 14 to 24-year-old, White, affluent, American males in laughs for hours. By the late nineties, Comedy Central emerged as a popular cable outlet for new humor. The station began experimenting with animation, most successfully with **South Park.** Kenny, Kyle, Stan and Cartman became anti-heroes for their crudeness and cynicism. This was pack of eight-year-olds, that cursed, manipulated, and talked-back with abandon. Parents were horrified that cartoons could present such disreputable role models but adults and parents soon learned that animation had evolved and was now targeting adult audiences and not children. Cartman's plan to gain weight, the weekly horrific murder of poor little Kenny ("Oh my God, they've killed Kenny, the bastards!" became a weekly slogan), the ridicule of prejudice towards controversial or different cultural figures like Mr. Jefferson (a thinly veiled reference to Michael Jackson's relationship to children) Big Gay Al, (a friendly non-threatening gay figure who befriends kids and even becomes a tolerable Scout master until the Scouts decide to bar him for his lifestyle), and the late Christopher Reeve (featured in a deeply disturbing episode about chronically ill people and the effects of stem cell research). Clearly, **South Park** pushed the envelope on what could be called comedy (a parody of Barbara Streisand had the singer transformed into a giant robotic figure, Mega-Streisand, resembling Godzilla). What it communicated to American youth was a challenge not to accept convention, to question the media, (even **South Park**) and not to become too comfortable in one's smug liberalism.

## MUSIC TALK

Beginning with the jazz era, musicians began to speak their own mystical language of form and content that was quickly picked up by music critics. Miles Davis and Gil Evans began to discuss Be bop and Coll jazz and free jazz. Critics like Leonard Feather and Ralph Gleason used to emulate these musicians in their writing about music for newspapers and magazines. Gleason, based in San Francisco followed the beat scene and quickly picked up on the young Jefferson Airplane, one of the formative bands of the San Francisco sound. In England rock critics made it fashionable to intellectualize the music of psychedelic rock and blend it with consumerist messages about enticing new bands and new sounds of the week. The British institution **Top of the Pops** played weekly hits and an appearance on the continually high rated show guaranteed extra sales. Even the Beatles dutifully performed on Top of the Pops. In America, beats, hippies, freaks, and musicians built a vocabulary of acceptance and protest that mirrored the anti-war movement. In **Rolling Stone,** rockers like Mick Jagger and Peter Townsend were beginning to wax philosophical about pop music and expressed theories about meaning and style movements. By the eighties, popsters in LA had created valley speak, and ghetto rappers were building their own musical language of slang and rap poetry.

### Rap: A Music Born in Controversy

Rap artists are continually evolving and arriving performing new forms of this expanding musical style. Sadly early rap innovators are quickly replaced by new heroes and the genre doesn't tolerate sitting still. In the late 80's The Beastie Boys, a group of New York white guys invaded a genre that was principally ethnic in origin and made it their own with innovative beats, slick production and a pop sensibility. Artists like GrandMaster Flash, Ice Cube, Run D. M. C., N. W. A., Jay-Z, Dr. Dre, Vanilla Ice, Tupuc, Tricky, Goldie, DMX, Destiny's Child and others have been quickly superceded by newer up and coming artists.

Rap has had a relationship with breakdancing, the avant-garde DJ scene, electronica, and soul music, but it has become most controversial for the use of profane language. Four letter words, rude commentary on females, and strongly antisocial sentiments are common elements. Parent groups have requested edited versions of controversial songs or parental advisory labels for CDs containing these lyrics. Rap is a cultural problem. It has been the centerpiece for lyric warning campaigns. Students who wear rap clothing, and listen to loud pounding music have been viewed as potential violence suspects. At times the rhetoric of rap has moved from the role playing fantasy play acting of hardened criminals to the actual practice of gunplay. These 'gangsta rappers' tote large weapons, entourages of bodyguards, and engage in a freewheeling, abusive, drug-centered life. Several years ago, two major rap figures, Notorious B. I. G. and Tupac Shukar were victims of gang violence and both died.

Rap music continues to evolve as a form with the rhyming and poetry becoming more complex and symbolic. But there is cause for concern when rap music lyrics inspire acts of violence or outrage. Eminem's song 'Stan' talks about the problems of hero worship. The protagonist, Stan, is writing to his rap hero because he thinks the music figure is as crazed as his lyrics. The fan is pathetic, hateful, and abusive to his girlfriend. He is angry at the rapper for not writing back. He eventually kills his girlfriend and drunkenly drives off a bridge. The rapper's belated return letter is a great reply. He just tells the fan to chill out and not take the music so seriously. "Before you hurt yourself, I think that you'd be doin' just fine If you'd relax a little. I'm glad that I inspire you, but Stan, why are you so mad? Try to understand that I do want you as a fan. I just don't want you to do some crazy shit." Even the rappers sense that impressionable youth can take the harsh rhetoric of rap as a lifestyle and not as simply a performance.

**Questions:**
1. Why is anti-social rap popular?
2. What does rap express?
3. What are some rap techniques that have moved to mainstream music?

# Film Speak: *Star Wars: Revenge of the Force:* 30 Years of Star Wars

The liberalization of the production code transformed how people spoke and communicated in film. Anger and hostility were popular when bonnie and Clyde hit the screen. Al Pacino (Serpico), Robert DeNiro (Taxi Driver) and Harvey Keitel (Mean Streets) opened the door to a new level of freedom in profanity expressing a crude but effective streetwise persona. Not just the words used but the subject matter changed as well. Homosexuality, violence, war, horror, and complex thought pieces were more often the subjects of big budget films. Films like Remains of the Day, American Beauty, and Chariots of Fire explored complex issues in complex terms.

In film, a dominate player for thirty years remained the **Star Wars Trilogy** which was joined at a second trilogy in the past six years. Though not as critically acclaimed as the first series of films, the second **Star Wars Trilogy** emphasized the life of anti-hero Darth Vadar, the series' most enduring and popular character. George Lucas returned as the director of the series and took critical hits for dull work with actors, but the series sputtered to life after the disappointing Phantom Menace with Attack of the Clones. Hayden Christenson made a strong-willed young Anakin Skywalker, and Ewen McGregor's vigorous Obi Wan Kenobi provided a strong older mentor focus. The series has brought several words into our vocabulary: The Force, the Dark Side, and the Empire. The worrisome thing is we hear these simplistic terms, terms taken from mythology and children's stories nearly mentioned with the same zeal in political circles and the dark side of outcome of Star Wars may be that it reduced political debate to the level of fantasy.

## Sources: Popular Culture

We forget that the humanities offer us splendid examples of communication. After all, what are tales and stories but examples of communication, sometimes old stories that were told aloud and written down. The greatest of the writers represented here also show us different forms of communication. Some deal with interpersonal relations, some with how we use communication to obtain knowledge, some deal with larger organizational communication.

### POLITICAL PERVERSITY: 20+ YEARS OF STRANGE ELECTIONS AND STRANGE ELECTORS

In the past 25 years the electorate has been increasingly volatile and uneasy with their choices for higher office. No where has this been more apparent in the range of odd political races for president over the past 7 or 8 elections. The results of each has been increasingly dubious and illustrates deep splits in the American voting population and wide ranges of the effect of the media on their judgment. What is clear is that much of what the electorate thinks is important only seems to be important for a very short shelf life and new issues continually push out the old issues infusing debate with a puzzling set of attributes that theoretically should or should not effect election outcomes.

If we journey back to 1980, pleasant and nice man Jimmy Carter had seemed, though bright and nice, unable to deal with the deep problems of the U.S. economy that was plagued by foreign competitors eating our auto and electronics industry and rising gas prices. He was defeated by Ronald Reagan who promised more freedom from taxes, government, and more ability to innovate. Though people felt better during Reagan's time in office, housing prices soared, interest rates reached 12 percent, and disparity between wealthy and poor people widened. Reagan preached "trickle down economics" that the Democrats pronounced "Voodoo economics." His theory was that tax money returned to wealthy Americans and companies would stimulate growth. In some instances it slowly did, and in other instances, the wealthy simply pocketed the extra cash.

By 1988, as the economy slowly rallied, the campaign between George Bush Sr. and Massachusetts governor Michael Dukakis became a race that the media dubbed between the Wimp and Shrimp. Dukakis was short and George Bush was seen as wimpy. Americans glowing from the Reagan

Photo courtesy of Library of Congress

years chose the wimp. Bush fought a successful war against Saddam Hussesin and seemed to be an easy victor in the 1992 race, but the economy turned sour. Bill Clinton, a minor Governor from Arkansas galvanized the people with his pleading expression, "I feel your pain," and extended empathy to the people. When President Bush was asked about rising prices at the checkout scanner, he had to ask reporters what a scanner was. Bush's family was so wealthy and powerful, he had not personally shopped for years, and had no idea what people were paying for food. He lost. Clinton became the most successful domestic president in thirty years guiding Americans to their highest standard of living since the sixties and narrowing the gap between rich and poor with modest tax breaks for middle income families, education incentives, a reduction in government, and an isolationist policy that kept America free from most foreign wars. In Somalia, 18 Americans died in the Blackhawk Down incident and Clinton pulled American troops out of the UN conflict in Somalia within a month. (Not before U.S. forces repaid the Somalian warlords by killing thousands of their hired mercenaries.) The Bosnian war was managed by sending in UN forces and General Wesley Clark secured a peace in the volatile region without the loss of a single American life. Clinton sent envoys to Ireland and Israel and nearly made a peace in both countries. At the last, Yassar Arafat and the Palestine Liberation Organization (PLO) pulled out leaving the deal to produce peace hanging.

Things looked bright. In the 1996 election Bob Dole argued that the press and film needed to be censured, but the issue never took hold. In congress, the Republican party swept to power in 1994 on the issue of term limits. They still hold complete power over Congress more than ten years later. The changes and cleanup they promised for a more moral and smaller government returning more money to the people has yet to happen. Their contract with America remains unfulfilled. In 2000, Al Gore was a dull campaigner and voters were angered at Clinton not so much for his successful governance of the country but for his stupid lies concerning an affair with intern Monica Lewinsky. George Bush, an untried governor from Texas ran on a campaign of less government and less taxes and was hit almost immediately by a stagnant economy and then the disaster of 911. A surplus turned to a deficit, the wars in Afghanistan and Iraq were costly in debt (over $200 billion dollars by conservative accounts), the use of National Guard troops and human lives (over 1600 Americans and contractors, and Amnesty International estimates over 100,000 Iraqi army and citizens, women and children killed). In 2004, Americans were less interested in the long (three years of two wars) battle, and the disappointing lack of outcome in finding suspected 911 perpetrator, and were more entertained by Swiftboat Veterans for Truth (a group that argued the five time decorated war hero and after the war, Congressional critic of Vietnam, Senator John Kerry, did not deserve his hero status) and social topics like abortion and gay marriage. The federal government had little control over abortion, gay marriage or the veterans. These were mostly either state law issues of media publicity items. In any case, a quieter more serious and conciliatory George Bush regained the White House in 2004 and the things remain much as they were for the past four years only fuel costs and housing costs have more than doubled.

What Americans vote for and why they vote at all (if they vote) has puzzled and troubled analysts for years. They don't seem to vote self-interest as much as ideology. Bravery, patriotism, morality, and digging in one's heels for supposed "issues" (gay marriage, term limits) seems to be more powerful than expecting government to have an actual role in keeping us safe, keeping us away from war, and keeping food on the table and a roof over our collective heads. In recent elections, immigrants seem to be taking a strongly conservative stand, and youth though vocal about their feelings don't seem to vote much at all. What American will be thinking in the next election is anyone's guess.

# Chapter 12

## Communication and Correct Format

### SPEAKING AND WRITING CONVENTIONS: MLA AND APA STYLES

#### Using the Web and Using Good Sense

Be careful when using the web. **Lots of information on the web is false or inadvertently wrong or out of date.** Since virtually anyone can create a website (even me . . .) there is no telling how reliable that data is. Further, there are no automatic checks on information submitted to the web. It is likely not reliable as financial, medical, or legal data. It's history or chronology can be flawed, and the editorial quality may prove to be ungrammatical and virtually unreadable. You'd be surprised how many bad web pages I have seen or read. Be careful of specific organizations that might represent certain bias. The American Family Association is a prime example. The names American and Family suggest a strong family oriented group but their recent front page attacks Kraft Foods for supporting gay groups, it asks for support for anti-flag burning legislation, it complains that condoms may be advertised on television, and it bemoans the Supreme court ruling on the 10 Commandments in public court rooms. Norman Lear's (the man who created All in the Family) People for the American Way Organization (which tells you who started their organization and WHY on the front page) follows such groups and labels the AFA a radical right wing organization. Some of AFA's stands seem extreme and have little or nothing to do with family issues and seem to be closer to right wing lobbying tactics. So beware if a web site labels itself as 'family' or anything that sounds WAY to friendly. It could be a site using questionable information. That's way it is always better to verify with books and magazines that you can touch and read. These were printed. They cost money to develop and they were usually edited by competent (if not always right. . . .) editors. Web sites aren't always so lucky. Just because someone has a website does not mean the information contained within is true. You will be held accountable if you quote that website and it is not true.

## Headers, Bodies, and Footers

Examine the header, the body and the footer of a webpage. The header should contain data about where the website is made and what type of website it is. The header contains the web address. Consider this address.

www.startrek.com

This tells you a great deal already. First, this is a Star Trek site related to the classic television series. The suffix com tells you it is a business. If the suffix was different you'd learn other things.

.net usually refers to a network or group
.gov usually refers to a government group
.com usually means a business of some kind
.org usually refers to some kind of organization
.edu usually refers to some sort of school or educational group

Other suffixes include country names. For example the suffix:

.uk refers to the United Kingdom including England
.de refers to Germany
.fr refers to France

For **academics** and for work in a colleges, professors tend to trust **academic** (.edu) sites **more often** than business sites. (.com) Usually this is based on the idea that a commercial site will likely have a **monetary** objective, but that an academic site will be more **impartial** in how it reports information. Academic sites might also like to make money but they are usually very forthright if they want payment for their information. Commercial information can be trustworthy but it can also be biased by product endorsements, marketing considerations and the framing of ideas.

**The body** of a webpage should contain:

Author information
Dates of composition
Bibliographies
An idea of where research was obtained
When the research was done
Why was the research done?
What is the site's purpose in existing?
Credentials of the authors and their perspective on issues.
A clear sense of the authors perspective on issues (does the author have bias?)

**The Footer** should include additional information such as:

The author's name and qualifications
The date of composition

The organization sponsoring the information
The page number or the word count of the whole article

It is probably clear from this discussion that **web writing suffers from several obvious flaws.**

The author is often unknown.
The organization sponsoring is unknown.
The information isn't numbered by page.
The information has no date of composition.
The purpose behind the writing is unclear.

## *Reliability and Credibility*

When quoting web sources consider these points:

1. **What is the authority of the author to make these points?** Does this person have a degree or any expert knowledge in the field they are writing about and is that knowledge that they gained from a trustworthy source. I might read an article by a Satanist but just because he spent 4 years in Satan Jr.'s academy doesn't mean I will likely believe that person's ideas. I would be more likely to believe an anthropologist with a degree from Harvard in Anthropology writing about Satanism.

2. **How accurate is the information?** What if the author uses horribly bad date, or wrong date, or out of date data? This might also make the writing unreliable. How old is data that is too old. When it is political or news worthy a week might be too old. If it is religious or historical, older data may be still quite reliable to quote.

3. **How objective is the author?** If the author fought for the confederacy during the civil war, that author might have a poor opinion of the union forces. This would be natural, but it would be highly unreliable for a portrayal of union forces in a textbook. We need to separate facts from opinion. Sometimes that is hard especially in news broadcasting.

4. **How current is the information?** Was the information produced recently? In medicine this can be essential to believing information. Old information can represent outdated beliefs and techniques. The same is true in the humanities.

5. **What is the coverage of this information?** Was the information intended for children? Who was consulted and who is the intended audience? Who was consulted in the creation of this information? Was that information found from a wide range of sources or only from one text? Usually more reliable information is based on multiple studies.

## USING THE MLA FORMAT IN WRITING AND SPEAKING

### Citing Sources in the Text

When you use or borrow information from an author or speaker you must insert a short text note when you quote or paraphrase that author's words or specific ideas. Generally, use text notes with anything you feel unsure is your own idea and an idea best described or ascribed to someone else. Text notes are easy and not difficult to insert. Usually the format is the author's last name and a page number like this.

In Beckett's play, **Happy Days,** he toys with the notion of the strange. What is strange for Beckett may not be strange for us. "No, here all is strange." (Beckett, 44)

This text note includes the author's name and page number. If you did not know the author's name and just the name of the work you would place the note like this. Just place the short title and the page number. If you lack a title or a page number place a note that gives a brief description of the work and the location within the work. Try to be accurate.

(**Happy Days,** 44)

For example, this text note: (*Buffy, the Vampire* episode, near the middle) is fairly worthless as a text note about a television show. But if you knew the show and the title of the episode, it is more helpful if still a little difficult to figure out. (**Buffy,** "Hush") At least now you've narrowed it down to a specific episode and a specific show. What if you are quoting a webpage with no page number, no author, and no title? This might help. (Buffy Fan Site, article on *Angel*) This is still short and the reader can find the address in the Works Cited. They hopefully can find the page you quoted in the navigation of the website. This shows how difficult websites are to use and rely on as research.

## CITING SOURCES

### Formats

Principle styles used for citing sources and writing scholarly papers are:

> MLA (Modern Language Association): Used for all publications in the humanities.
> APA (American Psychological Association): Used in all social science publications
> UC (University of Chicago): The style preferred by some high end academic journals and disciplines. The most complex esoteric format around.

Communication and Correct Format  155

Turabian, Kate. A Manual for Writers of Research Papers: Turabian's book has acquired legendary status over the years for its completeness and constant updates. It covers most other styles and is easily readable.

Some common source citing questions:

## How to Cite a Book

Maasik, Sonia, and Jack Solomon. **Signs of Life.** Bedford: Boston, 2000.

1. Flush first line to left margin. Subsequent lines reverse indent.
2. First author's name: last name first, the second author's name, last name last. Period.
3. Title of Book: underlined (or boldface or Italic). Period.
4. Place of Publication. (Usually only the city name is needed unless its from an unusual publication center. Like New York, Connecticut, would be an unusual publication source since many books are published in NY, NY. List the state in that case to avoid confusion with the more typical publication of NY, NY.) Colon.
5. Publisher's Name. Comma.
6. Date of Publication. Period.

## How to Cite a Website

Goetzman, Keith. "Playlist, Recommended Recordings." **Utne Reader** Online. 2 Nov. 2001. 4 Nov. 2001. http://www.utne.com/bMedia. tmpl?command=search&db=dArticle.db&eqheadlinedata=PLAYLIST%20107>

1. Just like a real magazine article only without page numbers and with an added internet address.
2. Author's name, last name first. Period.
3. Article title in quotes. Period.
4. Magazine title. Underlined. Period.
5. Date of magazine article.
6. Date site visited.
7. Internet article address in (< >) pointers.

## How to Cite a Film/Television Program/Video/DVD

**Ed Wood.** Dir. Tim Burton. Perf. Johnny Depp, Sarah Jessica Parker, Martin Landau. Hollywood Films, 1994.

1. The film title underlined. Period.
2. Director's name or the person most responsible for making it. Period.
3. The major two or three performers. Period.
4. Production company. Comma.
5. Year of release.

## How to Cite a Personal Interview

Senefeld, Dr. James. Personal Interview. 24 Oct. 2001.

1. Last name first of interviewee. Period.
2. Personal Interview. Period.
3. Date of interview. Period.

Many online guides exist to help students with MLA, APA, and Chicago.

*(Thanks to the Library Staff at Columbia State Community College for helping me to prepare these ideas. Ms. Margaret Anderson, Ms. Lyn Bayless, Mr. Rory Berry, Ms. Kathy Breeden, Ms. Karen Dearing, Ms. Jackie Egolf)*